Robert,
with best wishes

Paul Kelly
2/10/92

World Class Performance Through Total Quality

World Class Performance Through Total Quality

A practical guide to implementation

Paul Spenley
Director, Consultancy Division
Pera International, Swindon, UK

CHAPMAN & HALL
London · Glasgow · New York · Tokyo · Melbourne · Madras

Published by Chapman & Hall, 2–6 Boundary Row, London SE1 8HN

Chapman & Hall, 2–6 Boundary Row, London SE1 8HN, UK

Blackie Academic & Professional, Wester Cleddens Road, Bishopbriggs, Glasgow G64 2NZ, UK

Van Nostrand Reinhold Inc., 115 5th Avenue, New York NY10003, USA

Chapman & Hall Japan, Thomson Publishing Japan, Hirakawacho Nemoto Building, 6F, 1-7-11 Hirakawa-cho, Chiyoda-ku, Tokyo 102, Japan

Chapman & Hall Australia, Thomas Nelson Australia, 102 Dodds Street, South Melbourne, Victoria 3205, Australia

Chapman & Hall India, R. Seshadri, 32 Second Main Road, CIT East, Madras 600 035, India

First edition 1992

© 1992 Paul Spenley

Typeset in 11/13pt Palatino by EJS Chemical Composition, Bath
Printed in Great Britain by St Edmundsbury Press Ltd, Bury St Edmunds, Suffolk

ISBN 0 412 36120 5 (HB)   0 442 31636 4 (USA)

Apart from any fair dealing for the purposes of research or private study, or criticism or review, as permitted under the UK Copyright Designs and Patents Act, 1988, this publication may not be reproduced, stored, or transmitted, in any form or by any means, without the prior permission in writing of the publishers, or in the case of reprographic reproduction only in accordance with the terms of the licences issued by the Copyright Licensing Agency in the UK, or in accordance with the terms of licences issued by the appropriate Reproduction Rights Organization outside the UK. Enquiries concerning reproduction outside the terms stated here should be sent to the publishers at the UK address printed on this page.

The publisher makes no representation, express or implied, with regard to the accuracy of the information contained in this book and cannot accept any legal responsibility or liability for any errors or omissions that may be made.

A catalogue record for this book is available from the British Library.

Library of Congress Cataloging-in-Publication Data available.

To my wife and family

Contents

	Preface	ix
Part One	**Introduction to Total Quality Management (TQM)**	1
	Chapter 1 – Total Quality Management – worldwide effect	3
	Chapter 2 – The management methodology	10
	Chapter 3 – TQM principles	19
Part Two	**Implementation of TQM**	37
	Chapter 4 – The executive/management role	39
	Chapter 5 – TQM structure and top-down requirements	56
	Chapter 6 – Quality policy	71
	Chapter 7 – Measurement	76
	Chapter 8 – Quality improvement teams	85
	Chapter 9 – Education and training	93
	Chapter 10 – Involvement and commitment	107
	Chapter 11 – Supplier strategy	116
	Chapter 12 – Time to market	120

	Chapter 13 – Organizational design	128
	Chapter 14 – Summary	137
Part Three	**Tools and Techniques for TQM**	141
	Index	169

Preface

TOTAL QUALITY MANAGEMENT (TQM) –
A COMPETITIVE EDGE

In the context of the European and Western manufacturing challenge being set by the 'Far Eastern Machine', it is of critical importance that manufacturing competitiveness is improved in Western companies.

The ability to export successfully is becoming even more critical to the economic well-being of developed countries worldwide. The Japanese domination of the motor cycle and domestic consumer markets has had a significant impact on the balance of payments in Western Europe and the USA. All the signs are that Japanese companies are ready and able to enter other markets aggressively, through takeovers, acquisitions and off-shore manufacturing facilities.

In Western Europe, the creation of the 'Single Market' in 1992 has provided major opportunities for companies to increase their market share. Unfortunately, many companies in the West have shown an inability to succeed even in their market when faced with tough, well-organized opposition, such as that from the Far East. There is very little time left for Western companies to catch up – the challenge is becoming more fiercely competitive daily. The time to improve competitive edge may be too late for many companies, as the European frontiers are dismantled and the Japanese companies continue to build off-shore plants in Europe. For example, it is a fact that companies are increasingly being forced to achieve world class manufacturing capability in order to compete and, in many cases, survive. Also, these pressures are not restricted to manufacturing activities – they apply to service industry activities just as strongly.

The ability to respond to these domestic and worldwide challenges is the differentiator between survival and extinction. Total Quality Management (TQM) is the means to establish that differentiator in your company. Whatever your business, the principles outlined in this book are always valid, and so are the key actions that need to be taken.

Product or service?

There is an artificial view that all companies can somehow be divided into either manufacturing or service 'sectors'. In my experience, it is wrong to compartmentalize companies into manufacturing or service sectors: all companies are different whatever sector they are supposed to fit into and I have seen more fundamental differences between 'service' companies than between manufacturing and service companies.

In fact, the so-called service sector comprises businesses that are as diverse as any manufacturing versus service comparison. Similarly, many people consider all manufacturing companies to be the same when clearly, depending on their size, product and industry sector, they are as diverse as service sector companies. To make things even more complicated, manufacturing companies contain many 'service' functions, such as Finance and Personnel, which do not fit neatly into the so-called manufacturing area.

Fortunately, as far as TQM is concerned, deciding which sector your company belongs to is not important – it is not even relevant. The biggest single piece of advice I can give to a company in any sector is to ignore your label as part of the manufacturing or the service sector and get on with the implementation of TQM, following the basic principles outlined. Every company I have ever worked for or worked with has been different and, for successful implementation, the total plan has to be customized carefully to the particular company.

The problem is one of perception – perception that service companies have nothing to learn from manufacturing companies, for example. In practice, it is enormously beneficial to talk to other companies who are implementing TQM, whether they are in your sector or not. You will find that the problems they have encountered or are tackling are surprisingly similar from company to company. Beware of the people who would convince you that somehow a company in your own sector must be the model to follow – they may be following the wrong principle entirely!

Another perception is that it is somehow easier to implement TQM into a company that manufactures a product. This view is basically and fundamentally wrong; I do not subscribe to the view that TQM has to be implemented differently into the service sector than the manufacturing sector – it is absolute rubbish. In many cases, it is more difficult for manufacturing companies to implement TQM, because they already have an established quality system which is product-based. This is an absolute requirement of course, but it causes confusion when moving to the broader-based, more business-orientated Total Quality principles. I have seen some manufacturing companies struggle for a long time to get their staff to understand Total Quality principles simply because of the narrow focus on product quality. In service companies there is no such constraint and, in effect, there is a blank sheet of paper called Quality which in many ways makes for an easier management task.

The direction is clear – all the principles outlined in this book are totally applicable to your company, whatever your 'sector'. This book shows that it is the company processes which are improved by the application of TQM, by ensuring that everyone understands their role and has the culture and the techniques needed to implement continuous improvement. There is not a different set of principles for service companies. Implement TQM correctly and it does not matter what sector you come from; remember that there are no two companies the same anywhere in the world!

I am absolutely convinced, after many years of experience in implementing TQM into companies from both service and manufacturing sectors that the basic principles contained in this book are right. These principles need to be followed carefully, but with recognition that the implementation plans must be configured and tailored to the specific requirements of the individual company. My sincere thanks are due to my colleagues and to the people in the companies I have had the privilege to work with who really make these ideas work.

PART ONE

Introduction to Total Quality Management (TQM)

CHAPTER ONE

Total Quality Management – worldwide effect

It was not so long ago that the USA and the UK were dominant in world markets – mainly due to the post-war hunger for consumer goods such as motor cars, motor cycles, televisions, fridges etc. It is also true that goods made in Japan were synonymous with a poor or cheap quality image.

Today it cannot be disputed that the Japanese nation have achieved a position of superiority in many markets throughout the world. This has been achieved by reversing the early image of shoddy goods to that of quality goods attaining a universally accepted position in the market where Japanese goods are recognized as being 'quality products'.

This reputation for quality has enabled Japanese companies to increase market share at a rapid and enviable rate. For example, in the UK motor cycle marketplace, the Japanese invasion succeeded to the tune of an incredible 94% by the mid-1980s from a figure of less than 30% in the late 1960s. The figures in the motor car market were even more impressive whereby in the same period, their market share rose from less than 0.5% to the tariff-constrained 11% of the mid-1980s.

Of course, companies like Nissan have established successful manufacturing operations worldwide, in order to further increase their market share, and are showing the capability of totally dominating the automobile market worldwide by the end of this century. Their world-beating achievements are remarkable and it is essential to understand the reasons for the Japanese success in world markets – a success based on the application of Total Quality Management (TQM).

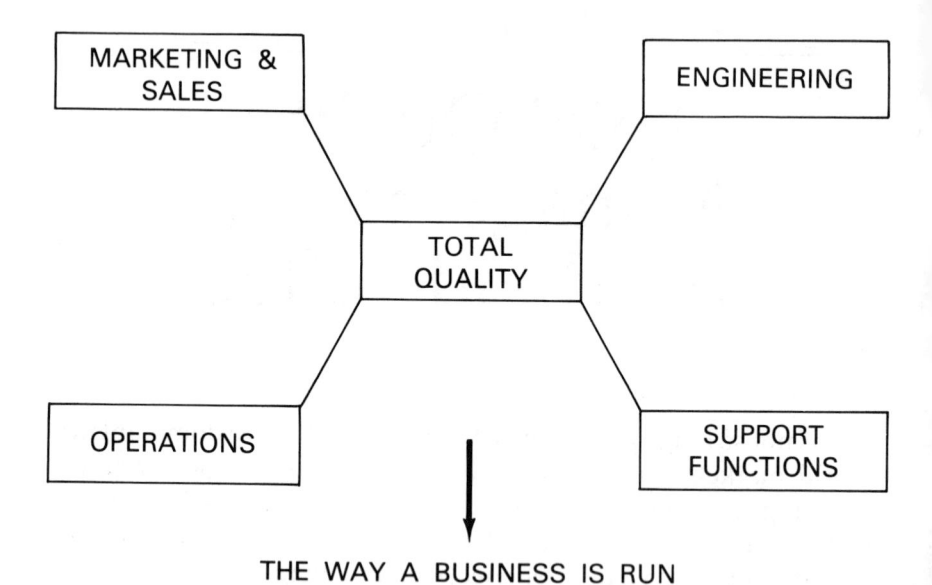

```
        MARKETING &                    ENGINEERING
          SALES

                       TOTAL
                      QUALITY

        OPERATIONS                     SUPPORT
                                      FUNCTIONS

                           ↓
              THE WAY A BUSINESS IS RUN
```

Figure 1.1 World class performance through Total Quality.

THE JAPANESE 'SECRET'

Immediately after the Second World War, Japanese goods had a reputation for shoddiness and cheapness that kept their competitive position in the bottom half of the world trade league table. This was mainly due to the devastation of their industrial base as a result of the war.

Also there was a management methodology modelled on the methods of F.W. Taylor who is often referred to as the 'Father of Scientific Management'. F.W. Taylor began his work in the early 1900s in the USA and could be said to be the world's first work study expert. He revolutionized work practices and productivity effectively by thinking of workers as 'human machines' designing the work equipment and expecting the workers to meet them without question. The only incentive for the workforce was considered to be their wage packets. This principle of management led to the use of piece-work payments and to the use of Inspectors to check output. This use of people as human machines revolutionized output, but at a reduction in the quality of output.

In the early 1950s, Taylor's methods were a fundamental tool in manufacturing industry worldwide and helped enable the USA to rapidly meet the huge post-war demand for goods such as cars or televisions. The Japanese recognized that they could not compete using the same Taylor management methodology but without the huge advantage the USA had in having an established industrial base, and began to develop an alternative strategy.

In the early 1950s, Japanese 'study tours' became a feature of many Western companies' lives, whereby the most successful companies were scrutinized in incredible detail in order to

Figure 1.2 The human machine.

define 'industrial best practice'. At the same time two eminent quality 'gurus' from the USA, Dr Edwards Deming and Dr J.M. Juran, were invited by the Japanese to help with the principles of quality control and their application in Japanese industry. This work formed the basis of a national drive, co-ordinated by the Japanese Union of Scientists and Engineers (JUSE), to improve quality control in Japanese companies which by the mid-1960s had achieved a cultural change in the methods and attitudes prevalent in Japanese industrial society.

Over the last 20 years the fundamental principles taught by Juran and Deming have been refined and built upon and applied with increasing success by Japanese companies. The outdated Taylor management principles have been replaced with a Total Quality management methodology where all employees receive education and training, and are encouraged and expected to contribute to the company objectives.

The establishment of the TQM methodology (or TQC, Total Quality Control, as it is referred to in Japan,) is the real secret of Japanese success. It has taken many years for the Japanese to develop and apply TQM. In many companies in the Western world, Taylorism is still the management methodology being used. The inability of many companies to realize that their management practices are the root cause of their lack of competitiveness in world markets is the key factor that will allow Japanese companies increasingly to dominate world markets into the 21st century.

QUALITY: A CULTURAL CHANGE – COMPANY OR COUNTRY?

There are many views on the cultural aspects of achieving TQM in a company. Some company executives feel that it is impossible to achieve a change in culture away from the old values of Taylorism to the new TQM total employee involvement principles. To support their rejection of TQM they point to the fact that the Japanese have a totally different historical culture from Western countries. Underlying this view is the absolutely un-

Figure 1.3 Company culture not country culture.

deniable fact (to them) that it is easy to manage the Japanese because 'they are used to doing what they are told'.

This explanation conveniently fits their current management thinking of 'telling people' – never asking – always viewing 'management' as experts. 'How easy it would be if all people would do as they were told.' The belief is that their Japanese managerial counterparts go round the organization telling their employees what to do all the time – the only difference is that the Japanese employees never question but do as they are told.

This view is defended most volubly by those managers who have never set foot inside a Japanese company or taken the trouble to study best management practice worldwide. It is a view that completely ignores the professional approach to the implementation of TQM that is adopted by successful Japanese companies. It also conveniently overlooks the fact that there are many Japanese companies who have also failed to successfully adopt TQM principles, but these companies are not successful and are therefore not known outside Japan.

How can the success of Nissan in Washington, County Durham, UK, be explained away as a country culture? This factory has successfully produced the Nissan Bluebird car to a higher quality standard than has been achieved in the equivalent

Japanese Nissan factory. The principles of TQM are the same whether it is an organization in Japan or in the UK, USA, Europe or any other developed country in the world. However, it would be foolish in the West to copy to the letter the application of TQM as in Japan. Much more time has to be spent in obtaining the understanding and acceptance of employees in the Western world in general, in order to obtain whole-hearted commitment. This is mainly because of the distrust and lack of communication between management and workers, built up generation upon generation by bad management practices, based on F.W. Taylor's principles of the early 1900s.

This atmosphere and culture cannot be removed overnight, but it can be removed over a period of one to three years, depending to some extent on the size of the organization, but mainly on management understanding and commitment. The culture of the company is set by the company, not by the country, more definitely it is set by the management of the company – no one else can have as big an effect on its employees.

TQM: A COMMERCIAL ADVANTAGE?

TQM is becoming synonymous with successful companies – it is increasingly being used as a public relations tool to persuade customers that the company can be relied upon to produce products and services that will meet customer requirements and therefore provide satisfaction.

There is no doubt that there are more TQM conferences, magazines etc. than ever and that there is a drive for many companies to be featured as successful TQM implementors in commercial and government publications. The danger is that some companies may want to jump on this particular bandwagon before a real TQM implementation has been achieved. If this is the case, it is inevitable that sooner or later the company will be 'found out', and will never get a second chance to take advantage commercially of TQM exposure even when implementation has been achieved. Those companies that are prepared to show visitors around their plants, and who are prepared to discuss failures as well as successes, are more likely to be TQM companies.

A quick and easy way to test TQM understanding is to ask a simple question:

How do you know you have TQM?
This question should be asked of the CEO or senior management and will generate a large number of responses!

The most definite answer I can offer is as follows:

- Every employee understands and is committed to the objectives of his department/area.
- Every employee knows who his intended customer and supplier is by individual name.
- Every employee has agreed requirements with his customer/supplier.

When this definition is understood in an organization, it is possible to audit and monitor the success of TQM by asking employees the relevant questions. It is even more revealing to use this definition to find out if a company, particularly a supplier, has TQM! This is achieved by asking the above questions of a secretary, receptionist, driver, goods-in clerk etc. Only then, will it be possible to check that management TQM claims are true!

CHAPTER TWO

The management methodology

TQM – THE WAY A BUSINESS IS RUN

'TQM is the single most important management methodology available today to achieve and maintain a competitive edge against worldwide competition.'

Put simply, there is little value in the Executive Board of a company arriving at a set of business objectives, for example to increase market share, introduce new products, increasing margins, reduce operating costs, implement flexible manufacturing systems or CIM, if there is no clear management methodology for achieving these business objectives.

This is not to deny the importance of setting clear business objectives through focussed market research or any of the other Business School and MBA methodologies that have been refined in the West over the past 20 years. Clearly all of the expertise that goes into providing a business strategy is of critical importance to the success of companies fighting on a world scale. There is no shortage of these skills in the Western world, indeed it has been suggested that there are more MBAs in one single American company (not named!) than in the whole of Japan. It would be wrong to assume from this that the MBA skill is not a valuable acquisition to a company. The need for a business strategy is of critical importance to the identification of key business objectives and the ability to fight successfully against competition worldwide.

However, what has been missing from Western companies,

Figure 2.1 The importance of everyone working together in the chain.

typically, is the utilization of a management methodology to implement the business strategy. TQM provides the management methodology which must form part of the total company business strategy, has been thought through, fully understood and implemented from the top down via the TQM process. This requires a fundamental change in culture for many companies in order to achieve a new and improved way of doing business. It is a corporate company culture where all employees understand what is required of them and are encouraged to contribute – as individuals and as members of Quality improvement teams – to the achievement of business objectives.

TECHNOLOGY

Technology when utilized fully and focussed to support business objectives can be a competitive advantage. Unfortunately it is very often the case in the West that technology has been utilized for its own sake instead of as part of a total business strategy.

It is a startling fact that in the period from the mid-1950s to the mid-1980s, UK scientists won 26 Nobel Prizes for scientific innovation, whilst the Japanese won only four. This is an enlightening statistic since the period is the exact time that Japanese industry successfully took major world markets. If technical edge was available to the West before Japan, why didn't Western companies take greater advantage? Again the answer lies in the inability of those companies to implement clearly their business objectives because of the lack of a TQM management methodology.

The Japanese were not misled by the exhortation to 'Automate or Die!' which was the clarion call in the early 1980s. Unfortunately this became 'Automate and Die' for many companies who, through poor implementation, failed to realize the benefits of their investments in automation.

It would be short-sighted to ignore the results of a survey conducted for the British Institute of Management (managing manufacturing operations in the UK 1975–1985) which showed that manufacturing efficiency improved only marginally between 1975 and 1985. It is foolish to ignore the fear that Western commerce and industry may fail to optimize the business benefits that the successful application of technology can provide. One of the problems is that technology is exhorted for its own sake by many people who are not directly involved with the running of a company.

Industrial leaders are rarely the champions of FMS, CIM, IT or other technology 'buzz words'. This mantle is taken on by consultants, academics, and of course the 'technical elegant expert', in companies – the people who like technology for its own sake 'if it moves, automate it!' Yet industrial leaders are the only people who can really make technology work, since successful application involves all the people in the organization. It cannot be left to technical experts – success depends on people's understanding, acceptance and commitment. Total quality management provides the management methodology for industrial leaders to harness the benefit of appropriate technology in line with, and as a key part of, implementing the business strategy.

THE HUMAN FACTOR

'Acceptance and understanding is a pre-requisite to obtaining whole-hearted commitment!'

If it were possible to obtain the whole-hearted commitment of every employee in pursuit of the company mission statement and business objectives wouldn't this be a factor in beating the competition? All successful sports teams demonstrate whole-hearted commitment – it is a major feature of a winning team. Why should companies be any different from sports teams and what is the differentiator that makes a company or a sports team world class?

The answer to this question fundamentally of course is its people. It is difficult to understand why so little attention is given to a management methodology that will achieve the whole-hearted commitment of all employees. The achievement of this objective is the most important aspect of a total company strategy. People are the differentiating factor between achieving world class capability and being also-rans. People are responsible for developing, implementing, controlling and maintaining the processes, methods and systems which companies use to provide products and services to their customers. To ensure these procedures, methods and systems work successfully it is essential that all the people fully understand the things they do, why they do them and of course help to specify, modify, implement and control their work.

It is necessary for each person to have an appreciation of his or her individual part of the total process and therefore of the effect this contribution makes to the total. This statement might appear crushingly obvious; it is hardly world shattering. However, it is my belief that the lack of understanding people have of their process as an integral and essential part of the total, is at the heart of inefficiency and a lack of competitivity in business. Examples are the design engineer who does not understand the requirement of designing a product that can be successfully put through the manufacturing process, the salesman who sells products that cannot be made, or the systems analyst who cannot understand the requirements of a factory stores manager – always assuming he asks him in the first place!

There are, unfortunately, too many examples of compartmentalization where the total requirement is not understood and when individuals do not understand or address their contributions to the total business needs. This compartmentalization can be seen in the functional 'Empires' built around design, manufacturing, sales, marketing and so on. Worse still, in some cases these functional empires begin to see each other as the competition instead of concentrating on the real competition! This of course is akin to shooting yourself in the foot before having to face the real enemy! There are no prizes for working out who wins.

What is needed is a methodology to ensure employees recognize the need to work for, and with, each other against a common enemy – the competition. This task is fundamentally a management role in providing the leadership and example for the rest of the employees to follow. It demands a common understanding of what needs to be achieved by the company, and a recognition that the company is the employees, all of whom have a key role to play, both as individuals and as members of teams. This requires all employees, as stated previously, to have a clear understanding of what they need to contribute as individuals and as part of a department, division or organization with clearly stated and agreed objectives.

If management understand the employees are the key to competitive advantage, then the old traditional barrier between management and employees will begin to be dismantled. The company is its employees whether they are called managers or not, and all have a vital role to play in achieving and maintaining competitive advantage.

COMMITMENT TO PEOPLE: THE KEY TO COMPETITIVE ADVANTAGE

In this chapter it has been highlighted that Western companies have successfully developed technology but failed to optimize a

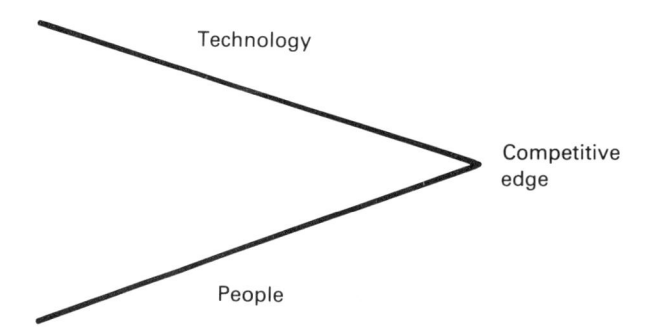

Figure 2.2 TQM links people and technology to activate the business strategy for competitive advantage.

business benefit. It is also true that they have developed many excellent business strategies but failed to implement these strategic plans successfully. The elements of a company strategy have frequently failed to include the third key factor – people. Without the understanding that people are a key factor in the implementation of the business strategy, companies will fail to achieve competitive advantage.

Indeed as technology and business strategies become more and more easily available to companies worldwide, the only differentiating factor will be the people.

BUSINESS REQUIREMENTS

By definition of the marketplace we expect in the 21st century, Western companies need to achieve world class capability.

Put simply, this means the ability to meet customer requirements better than the competition can. These requirements vary depending on the marketplace and the individual customer, but it is a fact that universally customers are demanding better quality of service, as well as quality of products. This means companies have to achieve competitive edge through business 'drivers' which reflect customer concerns.

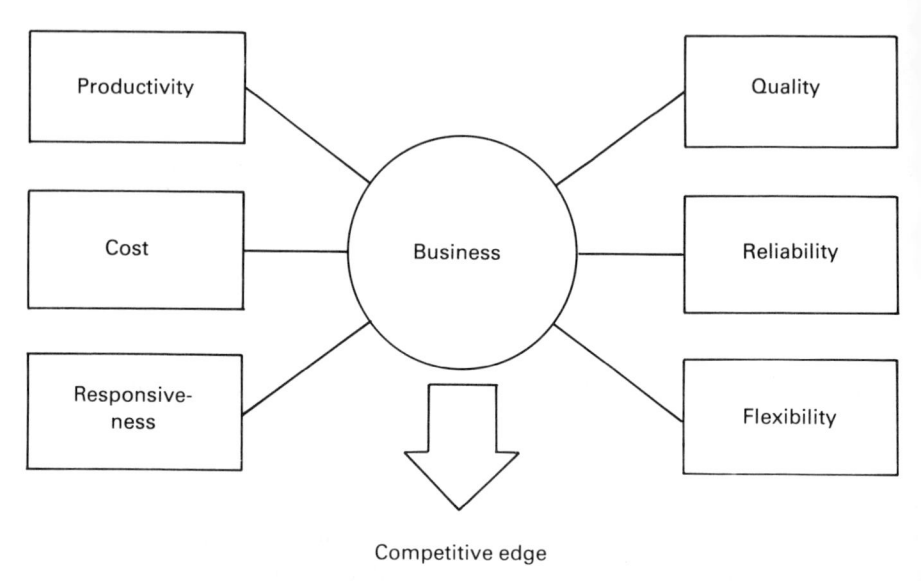

Figure 2.3 Business 'drivers'.

INVESTING IN PEOPLE

A good test of a company's commitment to investing in the people it employs is the training budget. Very often, the money budgeted each year for education and training is only a few per cent of the investment made in technology. This is akin to buying a Rolls Royce without bothering to learn how to drive! For example, the UK national average for 'off the job' training is about one-and-a-half days per employee per year. In Japan, the figure is in excess of ten days per employee per year. Most significantly, in Total Quality training, Japanese managers are given more training than the rest of the employees. This is to ensure that the management fully understand the TQM principles, tools, techniques and methodology, so that they are respected by the people who work for them and can make a personal contribution to the company quality improvement process.

It is important to understand that training in TQM is a con-

Company course	Trainees	Time	Outline of contents
Total quality basics	All new employees	½ day	What total quality is. How it is applied in the company. Quality improvement teams.
Quality assurance	All new professional staff	2 hours	What quality assurance means. How to assure quality (prevention). Quality assurance structure.
Tools and techniques	All employees	1 day	Tools and techniques. How to use. Problem solving process.
Total quality for supervisors	All people with supervisory responsibility	½ day	Role of supervisor. Team leadership.
Total quality for managers	All managers	1 week	Role of manager, quality assurance, team leadership, problem solving, tools and techniques.
Improvement team leader course	All team leaders	3 days	Role of team leader. Problem solving process. Tools and techniques.
Outside company courses	Assigned by managers	½ day to 1 week	Provided by external experts.

Figure 2.4 Japanese company TQM training schedule.

tinuous process for all employees and not a 'one-off' investment for a year. If this 'one-off' approach is adopted, then the TQM training will be seen as a programme, not as a process. It is essential to avoid the use of the word 'programme' because this indicates lack of understanding that TQM is a continuous improvement process. A programme has a beginning and an end – continuous improvement is never-ending.

Figure 2.4 shows a typical training schedule for Total Quality as practised by successful Japanese companies. It is a useful exercise to compare your company's Total Quality training with this schedule and measure the real commitment to the Quality Improvement Process.

CHAPTER THREE

TQM principles

SIMPLE PRINCIPLES

The principles of TQM are a set of commonsense beliefs that determine the individual's actions in everyday life – not just at work! It is a fascinating effect of TQM that individuals do apply TQM to their non-work lives, particularly when affected by poor service in a restaurant, hotel or transport. The reason for this is that the focus and awareness of quality is increased through the understanding and application of TQM principles and meaning.

Perception of quality

One of the biggest problems faced by a company in implementing TQM throughout the organization is the understanding of what is meant by the term 'quality'.

It is essential that the company has only one definition of quality which everyone can understand and that makes sense. Unfortunately quality means different things to different people. For example, the media, advertisements and everyday conversations portray quality as meaning 'excellent', 'luxurious' and 'expensive' – all subjective terms. The trouble with this concept is that quality means anything that you want it to! In business, quality is associated with 'quality control' – the inspection of people's work in order to make sure it meets the Quality Control Standards. This approach suggests to the people in an organization, that the only department responsible for quality is the Quality Control or QC department.

These definitions, or to be more accurate, perceptions, of what quality means to the people in an organization have to be changed. It is essential that everyone in the organization believes in one definition of quality and believes that quality relates directly to them, as individuals, and as members of a team. This is a challenge that has to be confronted head-on by management – it is no use taking the TQM implementation and calling it something else. In other words, leaving the word 'quality' out in order to avoid confusion with 'Quality Control'. I have been asked on occasion by company executives:

> 'I wish we could call this TQM something different, after all everyone thinks quality is about Quality Control, but what you are talking about affects the whole Company – it is to do with everyone.'

'It is to do with everyone' and that is precisely why it is necessary to change the perception of what quality means to the organization. What is there to be gained by keeping the old perceptions and meaning of quality? The answer is, nothing at all and the sooner that quality is re-defined to allow everyone in the organization to feel it relates to them, the better.

Quality needs can be defined simply as follows.

Quality means 'meeting agreed requirements'
Meeting agreed requirements between:

- individuals
- sections
- departments
- divisions
- companies

TQM is a tough discipline because it is not an easy matter to define requirements clearly, or to obtain agreement, much less to achieve those agreed requirements. It will take time even to get started on occasions – that is a definition of requirements, but what will be avoided is half-understood agreements, second

> **A little story**
>
> This is a story about four people named Everybody, Somebody, Anybody and Nobody.
>
> There was an important job to be done and Everybody was sure that Somebody would do it. Anybody could have done it but Nobody did it.
>
> Somebody got angry about that because it was Everybody's job.
>
> Everybody thought Anybody could do it but Nobody realized that Everybody would not do it.
>
> It ended up that Everybody blamed Somebody when Nobody did what Anybody could have done!

Figure 3.1 A little story.

guessing which lead to poor commitment and lack of achievement, as illustrated in Figure 3.1.

What happens as the TQM principles are spread throughout the organization, is that individuals begin to use a common language for 'quality'. For example, it is common to hear the words: 'My requirement is', instead of 'I think I need'. Defining quality clearly, simply and in a manner that enables everyone to understand what it means is the **first requirement** (to use the language!) of TQM implementation. The first principle of TQM is therefore:

> Quality means 'meeting agreed requirements'

Concept of internal customers and suppliers

Having understood what quality means it is necessary to consider the customer/supplier relationship. It is easy to understand

Suppliers → ☐ → ☐ → ☐ → ☐ → Customers

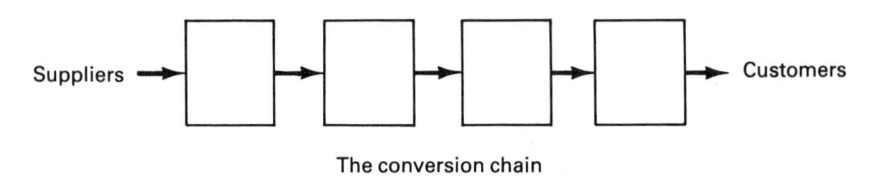

The conversion chain

Figure 3.2 Business is a chain process.

when the 'Customer' is the company buying your product or service. It is less easy to understand the concept of the 'internal customer'.

It is a fact that each person, whatever the process for which he or she is responsible, has a customer and a supplier. No one in an organization is exempt from this fact, even though some people might wish to ignore it! It follows from this straightforward fact, that each person is therefore both a customer and a supplier and has to recognize this in order to ensure the process for which he or she has responsibility is completed to the requirement. The simplest way to understand this is to ask two simple questions for every process that exists:

1. Who is my customer? (Do I have agreed requirements?)
2. Who is my supplier? (Do I have agreed requirements?)

This understanding of the chain-link interdependency of people in organizations is fundamental to achieving quality improvement. It is only as strong as its weakest link. The reason that achieving the business benefits is so difficult, is that it has to be understood and applied by everyone. Achieving this understanding is the greatest difficulty in implementing total quality successfully and within a realistic time scale.

BARRIERS TO UNDERSTANDING

What is the problem in understanding such a simple concept as the internal customer/supplier relationship? The answer to this is **attitude**! For example the attitude of a Marketing Manager when told that his customer is the Design Manager, or the attitude of a Design Engineer when told that his customer is a Production Shop Floor Operator.

Perceived status

The barriers are 'perceived status', compartmentalization, or sheer big-headedness!

'Do you mean to say that person is my customer?'
'Do you mean I have to speak to him!'
'Do you mean I have to ask him or her what he or she requires?'

The usual response is as follows:

'Not likely – I tell other people what to do!'

This status-conscious attitude is at the heart of the Western difficulties in successfully implementing the TQM Quality Improvement Process.

This conviction that management, and in many cases qualified professionals, 'know it all and have nothing to learn' is the root cause that will have the effect of destroying any TQM implementation process before it has begun. How can one person know and understand all the processes managed by all the people in the department or organization? How can one person be expert in all those processes? And most important of all: how can one person continuously improve all the processes in the organization at the same time!

The answer, of course, is that one person cannot, and that the person running the process must be the expert, whether it be a hotel receptionist running the process of booking guests in, or the secretary typing a letter, or a goods inward clerk booking in material from suppliers. Once management recognize that they have people working for them who should be experts in their job, the management role is clearly understood in terms of the customer/supplier relationship. It is to ensure that requirements are agreed and managed through communication, teamwork and management support. The realization that the manager has people working for him or her who are customers as well as suppliers is the key to good TQM management.

There is no room for the status-conscious manager who hides behind an office door and therefore breaks the line of communication to his people. How can there be a customer/supplier relationship where the customers aren't allowed to enter the shop! Each manager, each person needs to ask the question:

'What do I need to do to ensure my customer can do his or her job to the requirement agreed?'

This question does not take account of qualifications or status, only the requirements of the people in the company trying to do their jobs properly.

CONTINUOUS IMPROVEMENT ATTITUDE

The definition of quality 'Meeting Agreed Requirements', using the concept of the internal customer/supplier relationship is fundamental to the achievement of business requirements. However, business requirements never stay constant – competition is always there. Companies need to be constantly improving their service to customers, and developing new products to capture or maintain market share. It is a tough and ever-changing environment to work in and it is getting tougher and more changeable every day.

It is essential that companies recognize the importance of the process of continuous improvement in all areas and involving all people in the organization. It is hard enough to reach a situation where all people understand that quality means 'Meeting Agreed Requirements' using the internal customer/supplier concept. However, when those requirements have been met a new set of tougher requirements have to be agreed. Sometimes this is a tough fact to accept when a lot of hard work and commitment has gone into achieving a specific requirement, which may have been considered 'impossible' at one time. It is tempting to 'bask in the success' and forget that a new even more demanding set of requirements need to be agreed.

I believe that recognition of achievement and success is a key part of TQM, and will be discussed in a later chapter, but it is essential to recognize that after the celebrations, a new tougher challenge needs to be taken head on! This is the attitude of continuous improvement; not being satisfied with meeting requirements once, but improving all the time. I believe that when the continuous improvement attitude prevails in all the people in an organization, that organization is going to be, or is, world class already.

ZERO DEFECTS

When continuous improvement is the attitude in an organization, it is logical that the standard required for everyone is zero defects. However, it is important to understand that zero defects needs to be qualified by talking about:

'Continuous improvements towards zero defects'

In other words, although zero defects is the only acceptable error rate, it has to be achieved through a process of continuous improvement. It is a mistake sometimes made at the start of the TQM process to ram 'zero defects' down people's throats. This will quickly be used by the cynics to suggest that TQM is 'not real world', 'airy-fairy', 'a waste of time', or 'impossible'. They will argue that zero defects is beyond their process capability. This is an argument used very often by engineers, for example 'I can't design software with zero errors per million lines of code – you don't understand the process capability'.

The answer to this is to obtain agreement on the requirement for the product in the marketplace, which may not be zero defects! Then to ask the person 'When you have achieved this, are you going to continuously improve towards zero defects?' In other words, make sure you set and meet the requirements – and then continually improve, always changing the requirements towards zero defects. With the cynics it is useful to test their dual standards towards zero defects. For example, as a customer, they don't expect their pay-cheque ever to be wrong(!) and no one would ever allow a nurse to drop a baby. These are zero defects requirements.

Figure 3.3 TQM man.

Why don't some people apply the zero defects requirements to the work environment? It is an undeniable fact that learning and applying the TQM principles at work does lead to the very same application outside of work. When requirements are not met by hotels, restaurants, shops etc. it is sometimes clear that there is a case for TQM man!

PLANNING FOR PREVENTION

The process of continuous improvement requires an approach to situations, all situations, that can be best called Preventative. It is based on the belief that if something can go wrong then at some stage it will. The requirement is to think through fully the activity or process to be performed and ensure the necessary actions are taken to prevent things going wrong.

At this stage many people will say: 'I simply don't have the time to spend thinking things through to that extent'. This is one of the hardest principles of Total Quality Management to actually 'live' – precisely because of the huge and conflicting demands on people's time. The time pressure does not only apply to the CEO, it also applies to each individual in the organization. There is enormous pressure to 'fix' things that go wrong, the 'fix-it mentality'. It is rare that the root cause of a problem is identified and action taken to prevent the same problem occurring again. If you think about it, this is why people don't have time to apply preventative thinking and actions, it is a treadmill characterized by a 'fire-fighting', reactive management style. This approach needs to be changed in order that managers, in fact all the people not just managers, create more time to plan and prevent problems occurring in the first place. The elimination of root cause problems once and for all is a key requirement if the benefits of Total Quality Management are to be achieved.

All management meetings and all action plans should be focussed on eliminating root cause problems. A key question to ask and to keep asking is this: 'What are we going to do differently to ensure this problem never occurs again?' This question needs to be asked again and again until everyone fully understands the need to take specific actions to ensure the elimination of the root cause for ever. The challenge for management is to recognize that 'fixing' problems is not enough, and that time and training effort is needed to change from fixing to the preventative style.

Identifying and eliminating root cause problems

Western management typically have little knowledge of the tools and techniques which must be used to identify and eliminate root causes. This is in stark contrast to Japanese management who are taught tools and techniques – and, more importantly, apply them – to identify and eliminate root cause problems.

It is difficult to eliminate root cause problems; if it wasn't tough to do this it would already have been achieved. It is essential for management to realize very clearly that if they themselves do not understand the TQM tools and techniques and apply them, then there is no chance at all of fully achieving TQM business benefits. The attitude that problem solving techniques are only for the people that work for them is wrong. The use of analytical, easy-to-use problem solving tools and techniques in the board rooms of companies is a fundamental requirement of TQM.

If management are not prepared to believe this and get on with learning and applying these tools and techniques then the ability to achieve a competitive edge through TQM will be limited severely. Indeed it is almost certainly a waste of time and effort starting down the TQM route.

This book is only of value if these points are very clearly made, such that management understand what they need to do. The tools and techniques are covered in Part Three and apply to everyone in the organization through their involvement in Quality Improvement Teams (Chapter 8). The Top Team (Executive Board or Senior Management Team which, from now on, I will refer to as 'Top Team') must lead the application of tools and techniques as the first Quality Improvement Team, so the temptation for managers to skip Chapter 8 must be avoided! These techniques apply to everyone.

For example, the benefits of applying the cause and effect diagram to a major business problem is to identify clearly areas for corrective action. To show what this looks like I have included a Cause and Effect diagram (Figure 3.4) drawn up by the Board of Directors of a UK Company who very quickly learned and applied the problem solving techniques in this book to address a key business issue.

It can be seen from the diagram that there are many areas for improvement which have been clearly identified as having an impact on Top Team efficiency. One of the most important aspects of applying problem solving techniques at Board level is

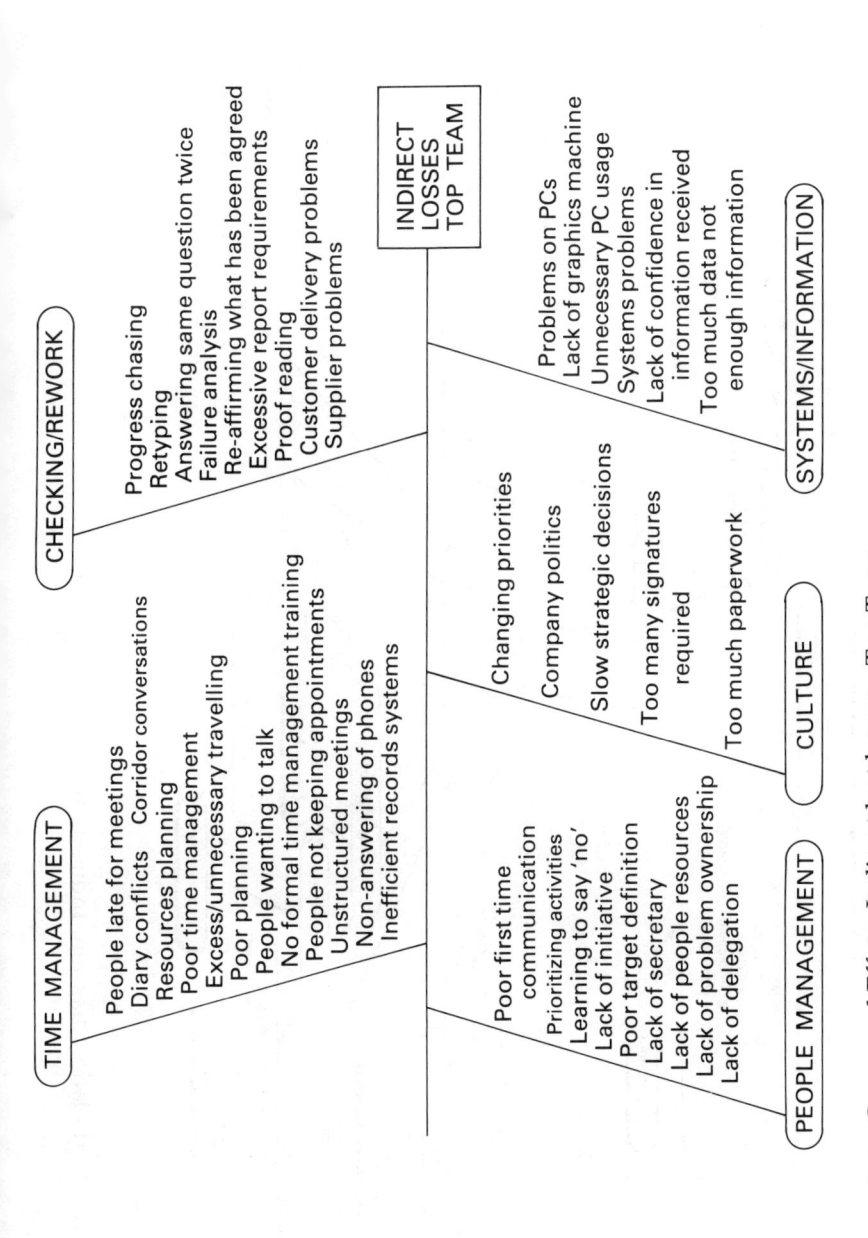

Figure 3.4 Cause and Effect. Indirect lost hours – Top Team.

TIME MANAGEMENT
- People late for meetings
- Diary conflicts
- Corridor conversations
- Resources planning
- Poor time management
- Excess/unnecessary travelling
- Poor planning
- People wanting to talk
- No formal time management training
- People not keeping appointments
- Unstructured meetings
- Non-answering of phones
- Inefficient records systems

CHECKING/REWORK
- Progress chasing
- Retyping
- Answering same question twice
- Failure analysis
- Re-affirming what has been agreed
- Excessive report requirements
- Proof reading
- Customer delivery problems
- Supplier problems

PEOPLE MANAGEMENT
- Poor first time communication
- Prioritizing activities
- Learning to say 'no'
- Lack of initiative
- Poor target definition
- Lack of secretary
- Lack of people resources
- Lack of problem ownership
- Lack of delegation

CULTURE
- Changing priorities
- Company politics
- Slow strategic decisions
- Too many signatures required
- Too much paperwork

SYSTEMS/INFORMATION
- Problems on PCs
- Lack of graphics machine
- Unnecessary PC usage
- Systems problems
- Lack of confidence in information received
- Too much data not enough information

INDIRECT LOSSES TOP TEAM

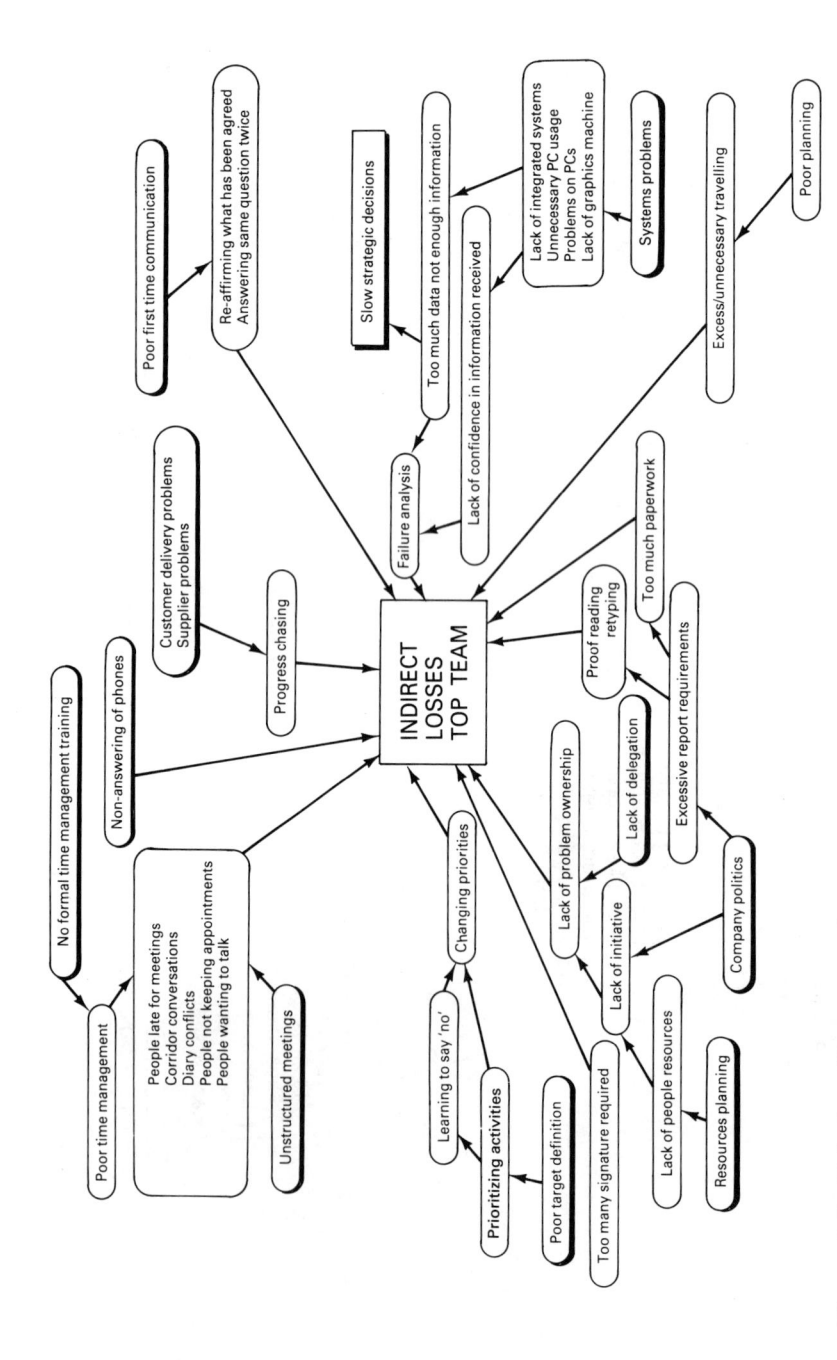

Figure 3.5 Relation diagram. Indirect lost hours – Top Team.

that all the Board members realize the total interdependency they have between each other. This approach also promotes 'consensus' management in the organization. For example, there is no problem in deciding on the need for corrective action teams combining people from different departments to be formed in order to solve a problem like poor Top Team efficiency.

Resources are more easily made available and there is no negative reaction to the request for individuals to spend time on problems which were not previously seen to be anything to do with their department. It is essential for senior management to fully understand the principle of prevention, learn to apply problem solving techniques themselves and ensure sufficient time and attention is allowed for the identification of removal of root cause problems.

If this is not understood, the company will never get off the 'fix it treadmill' – where the same problems keep recurring and the same fixes keep being applied – very often by different people. To avoid the treadmill, it is necessary to ask the same question whenever a problem is 'fixed':

'What are we going to do differently to ensure this problem never occurs again?'

COST OF TOTAL QUALITY

Cost of Total Quality is the concept of measuring, in financial terms, both the cost of failure and the cost of prevention. The cost of failure is normally termed the Cost of Non-Conformance (CONC). The cost of prevention is normally termed the Cost of Conformance (COC). Combining the Cost of Conformance and the Cost of Non-Conformance adds up to the Cost of Total Quality for a Business.

> COST OF TOTAL QUALITY
> = COST OF CONFORMANCE PLUS
>   COST OF NON-CONFORMANCE

The precise definitions are:

Cost of Conformance
The cost of investing to ensure activities are achieved to the agreed requirement and problems prevented from occurring.

Cost of Non-Conformance
The cost incurred by failing to achieve activities to the agreed requirement.

The Cost of Non-Conformance in most Western manufacturing companies is typically between 15% and 25% of turnover, but in service industries the figure is closer to 40% of turnover.

It is possible to clearly identify where non-conformances are occurring and to establish an analysis of those costs in financial terms. The details of how this is done are covered in Chapter 7, but Table 3.1 indicates generic areas found in a manufacturing environment. It is essential to understand that this is total cost of

Table 3.1 Areas in a manufacturing environment

Immediate loss	**Lost opportunities**
Scrap	
Obsolete stock	Excess inventory
Excess test cover	Poor delivery
Direct rework	
Indirect rework	
Warranty	
Debtors	

In service activities, there are corresponding costly areas of non-conformance.

Immediate loss	**Lost opportunities**
Direct rework	Discounts
Indirect rework	Excess stationery
Compensation payments	
Excess checking	
Overpayment	

quality and it therefore applies to everyone in the organization – not just the shop floor.

It is necessary to establish requirements clearly across the business and to measure when those requirements are not being met. The Cost of Non-conformance is a methodology for putting a financial measure on failure by measuring wasted time or wasted material. It is important to define a standard method for measuring Cost of Quality, this will then become the method for assessing financially the effect on the business of the TQM Quality Improvement Process.

It is normal for companies investing in TQM to initially increase the total Cost of Quality before a reduction is obtained. This is because finance is required for education and training and time has to be made available as an initial investment to give momentum to the TQM process. A typical total Cost of Quality trend is shown in Figure 3.6.

It has been proved by the author and his team in client companies that a reduction of between 2% and 5% of turnover can be achieved within the first year, when the TQM implementation methods in this book are followed. This has resulted in millions of pounds being saved providing returns on investment

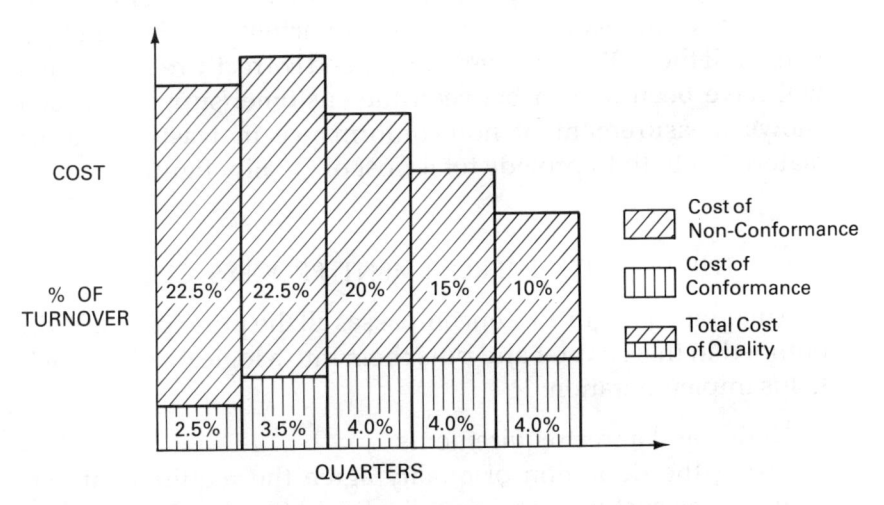

Figure 3.6 Typical cost of quality trends.

often exceeding 500% in the first year! Figures like these make it an easy task to justify expenditure on TQM, but care must be taken to ensure the total Cost of Quality system applied is credible and easy to use.

It is essential to avoid 'analysis paralysis' where the thinking is that it is better to be precisely wrong, rather than approximately right. In other words, don't try to apply total Cost of Quality to the last three significant figures – all the effort will go into recording the information and there will be no effort left to solve the problems. A set of rules must form the basis of the system to be used at all times, thus ensuring all improvements are calibrated against a fixed standard.

It has been more difficult for service industries or, to be more precise, non-product areas to measure total Cost of Quality. This is because manufacturing businesses producing a product have usually put in measurement systems for that product. However, even in manufacturing companies the non-product areas like Finance, Personnel, Sales and Marketing have found difficulty in applying total Cost of Quality methods. Again this is because a lot of the work done in these areas involves no direct product output.

The methods applied by the author have been proven to work in all areas of a company because they are independent of product. They are related to the process or activity carried out by a person. If the TQM principles are applied correctly requirements will have been agreed between the customer/supplier, which allows measurement of non-conformance in wasted time or material or both to provide total Cost of Quality figures.

THE QUALITY IMPROVEMENT PROCESS CYCLE

The diagram in Figure 3.7 encompasses all the principles of TQM outlined in this chapter and puts them into a logical order which helps implementation:

1. Define and agree requirements
   Using the definition of quality agree the requirement between the customer and supplier by asking the questions:

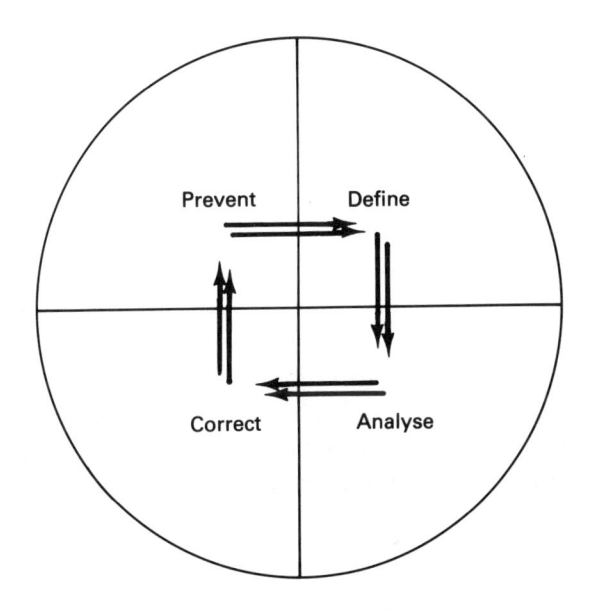

Figure 3.7 The improvement process cycle.

- Who is my customer?
- Who is my supplier?
- What requirements have I defined and agreed?

2. Measure non-conformance
Having a measurement system to establish when the process is not meeting the agreed requirement and applying a financial measure – the Cost of Non-conformance. Ask:

- Do I have a means of measuring non-conformance?
- Do I have a means of measuring non-conformance financially?

3. Apply corrective action
Using the non-conformance measures established to correct the problem by implementing a permanent cure – often termed a fix. Ask the questions:

- Do I know what the problem is?
- Do I need help to fix the problem or can I fix it myself?

4. Apply prevention system
   Ensure the problem <u>never</u> occurs again by considering
   - What process, method or system have I changed to ensure this problem never occurs again?
   - What are we going to do differently from now on?

This closes the cycle and takes us back to re-defining the requirement because requirements never stay constant; the competition is always improving and competitive requirements get tougher all the time.

This is the Process of Continuous Improvement, always tightening the agreed requirements, always eliminating error and going around the Quality Improvement Cycle again and again like a spiral until zero defects are met in the centre.

    That is the Quality Improvement Cycle

PART TWO

Implementation of TQM

CHAPTER FOUR

The executive/ management role

Without the commitment of top management to TQM, there is absolutely no point in a company adopting a Quality Improvement Process. The first time a manager stops one of his people from attending a Quality Improvement meeting, or a Quality training course, all credibility will be lost. Similarly if a manager allows a product to be shipped knowing there is a problem, if typographical errors are accepted, if meetings discipline is poor, with managers arriving late or poorly prepared, then all these events will prove to the employees that management is not committed and nothing will change in the organization. Indeed, if TQM is ill-conceived and poorly managed, this will lead to an even greater divide between management and employees and do immense harm to the Quality Improvement Process. In short, management and Quality will be a 'sick joke'.

It is critically important that top management take the time out to fully understand TQM and what it can achieve for the organization, and develop an agreed (at board level) plan for implementation before attempting to implement the plan. This will require these very busy people to make time available, <u>it cannot be delegated</u>. Clearly before the top management in a company will commit to making time available for TQM it is necessary to answer the question 'Why?':

'Why should I spend 2 hours a week in a TQM meeting?'
'Why should I spend 2 or more days on a TQM training course?'
'Why should I attend this TQM Conference?'
'Why should I read this book?'

'I Don't Have The Time'

What this response means is that management don't have the time to improve the way the business is run. This attitude is characterized by short-term thinking and long-term extinction (or even short-term extinction).

The attitude of top management to TQM must be demonstrated whole-heartedly, every day and in every action. Especially the messages given from Top Team meetings and decisions must show the positive commitment to TQM. This must start with a clear statement of 'Quality Policy' which encapsulates the ethics and values of the company. The CEO will lead the thinking on the Quality Policy statement, as described in Chapter 6, but the Top Team must contribute and

Figure 4.1 'Just keep driving the car – don't look to see if there is a disaster ahead by reading the map!'

agree a consensus statement. This will be a vision of what the company philosophy is – and should be.

Starting from this general vision, it is possible to assess the company's current standing and to determine the necessary approach in all aspects of business. Particular aims must be expressed in a 'mission statement', to focus attention from everyone on the specific goals set by the Top Team for the organization. The approach defined by the Quality Policy statement must lead the Top Team to implement TQM from themselves and down through the organization until everyone is involved and committed.

Quality of management

The quality of management in a company is directly linked to the quality of the business. By definition it is the managers' role to

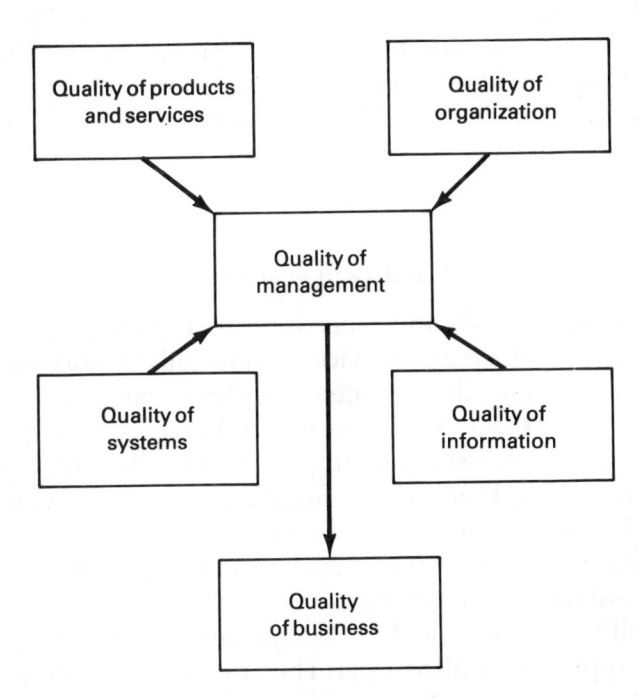

Figure 4.2 Quality of management.

manage the business – it is nobody else's responsibility. For example it is management who determine the quality of information, the quality of systems, the quality of organization and therefore the quality of products and services which determine the quality of the business.

Quality of information

Each manager should ask the following question: 'What information do I need to run my business?' If he isn't getting the information in the form required then it is his job to specify his requirement clearly. In this way it is possible to make a clear distinction between data and information. What is the use of receiving paperwork which in one week can take up most of a manager's desk? Many managers complain about the amount of paperwork but few actually do something about it. The rule is that only useful information which has been specifically defined as a requirement should be received. This will have a dramatic effect on the quality of information received by management, but of course management have to make the rules in the first place.

Quality of systems

The systems, methods and procedures that a company employs to output its products and services are critically important. However the definition, development, implementation and control of these systems is a difficult task and the ability to implement new systems successfully is important in achieving business requirements and thereby maintaining or improving a competitive edge. Management have a task to ensure that the correct methodology is used to implement systems to ensure continuity throughout the organization.

The following Total Quality Management methodology is universally applicable to all aspects of business from design through to distribution, but has to be rigidly applied.

The three-step requirements methodology
Step 1   Analyse and define existing system
Step 2   Specify completed system
Step 3   Phased implementation

This methodology is an essential element to the successful implementation of new and improved systems, methods and procedures in a company. The reason for this is that traditionally understanding of existing systems comes from either the written word which is often imprecise and requires a large amount of time to interpret, or through discussion which depends on interpretation, personal relationships etc. These difficulties in communication lead to inaccurate specifications for new systems which in turn lead to implementation and continual operational difficulties.

Integrated systems are particularly prone to communication difficulties as the areas for application are devolved into the operational parts of the company. The personnel in the operational areas need the opportunity to specify their requirements clearly. It is management's role to set the rule that through the TQM three-step requirements methodology, the operation of an existing system is clearly defined through the people who are the users. Also the new system is designed with clear understanding and involvement with the users. Finally of course, the new system needs to be implemented in a phased manner by the users, who fully understand each phase of implementation.

It is management's responsibility to set the rules – in this case the critically important use of the three-step requirement methodology to ensure successful implementation of new processes, systems and methods.

Quality of organization

Organizational change is often an area of concern for many companies, seen from the employees' point of view. Management changes can sometimes be seen as 're-arranging the deck chairs on the *Titanic*' for all the good they do. In fact, too many management changes can cause a feeling of instability and division in an organization.

In some organizations, even senior management are not made aware of the organizational changes; this breeds a feeling of resentment and instability which then fuels their employees' fears and concerns. The Total Quality approach to organizational change demands that the people are informed clearly of the changes and why they are being done.

The level of involvement in the organizational change decision-making process needs to be reviewed critically. An improved organization change without even management consultation will not provide an atmosphere where change and flexibility is welcomed – indeed it will provide totally the opposite. Certainly the Top Team in a company or division should be involved in the decision-making process and this should not be automatically decided and declared by the CEO. One of the key Japanese secrets of success is their commitment to 'consensus management'. This is common sense – if you are not involved in decisions which affect your way of working, then how are you going to show commitment? If this approach is adopted in the Boardroom, then it will also be adopted within the organization at each level. Again this approach to the Quality of the organization is a management responsibility.

Quality of products and services

'Management have a responsibility to recognise that the quality of products and services is what makes the company profitable and that everything that is done in the organization must be to support this ethic.'

This statement is simple and obvious, but it is often surprising that many companies lose sight of this fact and concentrate on internal issues which may have no impact on the customer at all. Sometimes a company will be 'Output Focussed', and 'Quality Blind'; it is management's responsibility to re-focus on customer requirements; to be specific, on the quality of products and the quality of service. Total Quality Management is about all aspects of the business, not just the products that are output; it is also about the 'Quality of Service' offered by the company.

The quality of service is determined by the quality of the people in the organization. Their attitude to the customer, and whether that customer is internal or external is critical to the achievement of a Total Quality culture in a company. For example, how many times will you wait for a telephone to ring before giving up and going elsewhere for better service? If you manage to get through and the person on the other end of the phone is unhelpful or surly, it doesn't matter how good the company product might be, the odds are you will go somewhere else.

Management need to recognize that quality is not just about products, but also about the quality of service offered by the company. This is much more difficult to achieve that product quality because it is all about people's attitude to the company and customers.

'Management leadership is the key'
This means ensuring all employees understand and are committed to what is required of them to ensure the company is successful, meets its mission statement and business requirements and therefore achieves and maintains a competitive edge.

MISSION STATEMENT AND BUSINESS REQUIREMENTS

It is essential that all employees understand the question: 'What business are we in? The answer needs to be encompassed within a clear, concise and short mission statement.

The elements of the mission statement may include:

Markets	: World, European, etc. segmentation
Technology	: High, low, product, specific
Customers	: Both internal and external
Quality of service	: Meeting requirements
Profitable growth	: Need to meet financial targets

```
"TO BE RECOGNIZED AS THE LEADING
INTERNATIONAL SUPPLIER OF ............
...................................
BY CONTINUOUSLY IMPROVING OUR
PRODUCTS AND SERVICES TO MEET OR
EXCEED OUR CUSTOMERS' EXPECTATIONS"

                SIGNED ....................
                         MANAGING DIRECTOR


              OUR ROLE IS:
  "..................................
   ..................................
   .................................."


                SIGNED ....................
                         DEPARTMENTAL TEAM
                       ....................
                       ....................
                       ....................
                       ....................
                       ....................
```

Figure 4.3 Typical mission statement.

A typical mission statement may read as shown in Figure 4.3.

The means of arriving at a relevant mission statement is critical, the requirement being that all members of the Executive Board or Senior Management Team – the 'Top Team' – agree and are committed to it.

The mechanism for achieving an agreed committed mission

statement is for the Top Team to brainstorm and then agree. Brainstorming allows each member of the team to put forward his or her statement in turn. In this way the key elements are agreed by the Top Team and within 2 hours or less it is possible to achieve the objective – i.e. a clear, concise and agreed mission statement which answers the question 'What business are we in?'.

The importance of all members of the Top Team agreeing the mission statement cannot be underestimated. By using the brainstorming method, each member has had to think it through and will therefore fully understand and be in a better position to communicate down the organization. Of course, a further advantage is that all members of the Top Team will be giving the same message!

Business requirements

If the Top Team is successful in achieving an answer to the question 'What business are we in?' then the next logical question is 'What do we need to be good at?'. This is what is meant by the business requirements, i.e. what does the company need to be good at in order to achieve and/or maintain a competitive edge. These may also be called Business Drivers, as shown in Figure 4.4.

The elements were discussed in Chapter 2, but it is worth reiterating that flexibility and responsiveness is determined largely by the flexibility and responsiveness of all the company employees. In communicating the mission statement and business requirements it is essential that this simple message is given.

Competitive analysis

Having established answers to the questions

1. 'What business are we in?' (Mission statement)
2. 'What do we need to be good at?' (Business requirements)

```
          Productivity                    Quality

                        \        /
                         \      /
            Cost ───── BUSINESS ───── Reliability
                         /      \
                        /        \

         Responsiveness                   Flexibility
                              │
                              ▼
                       Competitive Edge
```

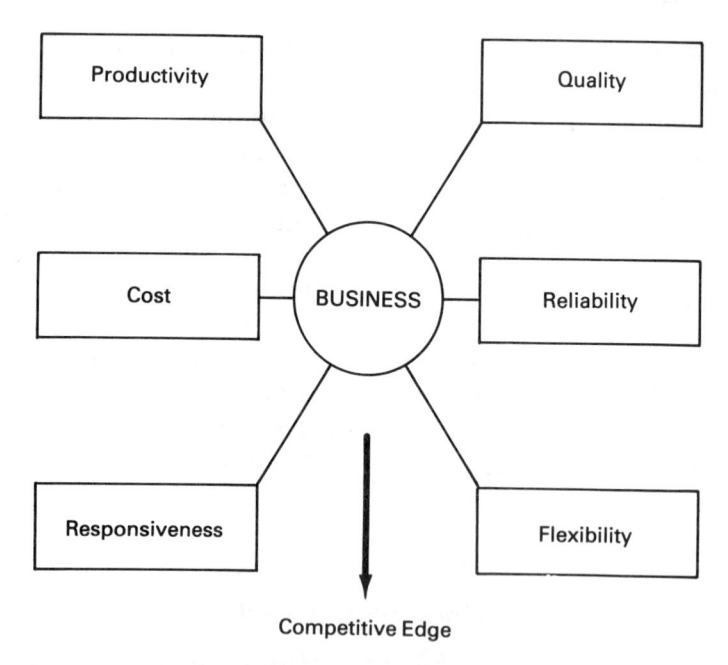

Figure 4.4 Business requirements.

the next logical question to ask is

3. 'How good do we need to be to achieve our mission statement?'

In simple terms this means being better than the competition and being perceived by the marketplace as being the 'Market Leader'.

The temptation is to use Total Quality to make exhortations to people to be 'excellent' or 'the best', or worst of all 'perfect'! This is an entirely useless approach since it does not provide specific targets – measurable, monitorable and achievable – which all employees can understand and be committed to. It is not necessary to be 'Perfect' to achieve a competitive edge, it is necessary to be better than the competition!

In order to find out how good it is necessary to be, the requirement is to complete a competitive analysis, benchmarking the company against the competition. It is useful to use the generic business requirements to establish quantifiable performance measures. A matrix can be used to establish the measures which might include cost, product quality, reliability, flexibility, responsiveness, productivity and so on.

Competitive Benchmarking

Having established the measures, it is necessary to obtain performance figures against the competition – benchmarking the best of the competition and establishing that measure as the standard to beat. For example, a typical benchmarking table is shown in Figure 4.5.

Customer Audit

A useful method for obtaining this benchmark information is to conduct a Customer Audit which can be used to establish competitors' capability as well as your own company's capability.

Most customers are happy to give information on competitor performance – after all, this can only benefit them! A typical questionnaire is shown in Figure 4.6.

Many companies use external agencies to complete the audits which can be valuable, particularly in assessing competitor performance. The use of a questionnaire has to be considered where there are many different customers, perhaps in different countries where it is impossible to visit all customer premises.

It is important to spend some time, however, considering how to ensure a good response rate to the questionnaire. An introductory letter accompanying the questionnaire and explaining its importance to the company and the customer is essential if the questionnaire is not going to decorate the rubbish bin!

A typical letter is shown as Figure 4.7.

A further requirement is to establish, whenever possible, a named person to send the questionnaire to. Although this will take more time and money, it is most likely to be successful in establishing a two-way dialogue between the company and a real customer.

Performance measure figure	Own company	Competitor A	Competitor B	Competitor C	Best practice
Time to market	14 weeks	5 weeks	20 weeks	12 weeks	5 weeks
Delivery performance	95%	90%	96%	93%	96%
Response time to orders	5 weeks	3 weeks	4 weeks	2 weeks	2 weeks
Reliability (time to failure)	1 year	2 years	6 months	9 months	2 years
Delivered quality	95%	98%	99%	96%	99%

These figures need to be constantly reviewed by the Top Team, to ensure improvements in Competitive Performance are noted and the benchmark updated accordingly.

Performance measure	Actual	Target	Competitor A	Competitor B	Competitor C	Best practice

Figure 4.5 Typical benchmarking table.

Supplier name	Regularity of contact with Director/Sn Mngr	Delivery performance on time	Quality of service (style/courtesy)	Technical quality of product/service
A				
B				
C				
D				

Figure 4.6 Customer audit questionnaire.

> Dear
>
> **CONTINUOUS IMPROVEMENT POLICY**
>
> It is our policy to continuously improve the quality of the service we provide to our customers. We are honest enough to admit that we do not offer a perfect service at all times, but we do not attempt anything less than 100%. However, we appreciate that this will take a lot of dedication, effort and commitment. We need to have increasingly close contact with our customers to enable us to improve our service to their benefit.
>
> By working with us you will help us to improve our services continuously – this questionnaire is designed to help us help you.
>
> Thank you for your co-operation.
>
> Yours

Figure 4.7 Continuous improvement policy.

Having established a name or names in the company this potentially allows for the establishment of 'User Groups' reciprocal visits and so on, all of which will help to create a customer supplier relationship based on a mutual understanding and trust. This in turn creates loyalty and is a key requirement in fending off the competition; in other words, what is often called 'Brand Loyalty'.

It is important to establish an honest and open relationship with customers where, although problems do occur between the supplier and customer, the customer understands that through his feedback, the service that is received is continually improved. There is no company in the world that is perfect. The successful companies are those that are committed to a policy of continuous improvement and it is impossible to achieve this if you don't talk to – and most importantly <u>listen to</u> – your customers.

OBTAINING COMMITMENT TO BUSINESS REQUIREMENTS FROM ALL EMPLOYEES

'Acceptance and understanding is a pre-requisite to obtaining the whole-hearted commitment of all employees.'

Having established the mission statement, business requirements, performance measures, competitive position, and customer feedback, there is sufficient information to begin communication to the total company. The content of the communication will follow this structure:

1. What business are we in?   : Mission statement
2. What do we need to be good at?   : Business requirements
3. How good do we need to be?   : Performance measures required
4. How do we stand against the competition? : Benchmark results
5. What do our customers think of us? : Customer audit information

It is essential to specify clearly the performance measures required to beat the competition and to underline the importance to all the company employees (including management as employees!) – of achieving a competitive edge.

Communication methodology

This information should be given to the total workforce at least twice per year. Management should develop information, updating answers to the basic questions set out above, which is presented to their teams quarterly allowing questions and answers. Team briefs should be given using the CASCADE principle illustrated in Figure 4.8 to monthly briefs of each departmental or divisional team. Feedback through questions and answers is an essential part of this process and must be built-in to each briefing session.

FULL REVIEW OF MEASURES

Having established the performance measures required to be competitive, it is essential to complete a top-down review of measures within the company. All these measures are only of

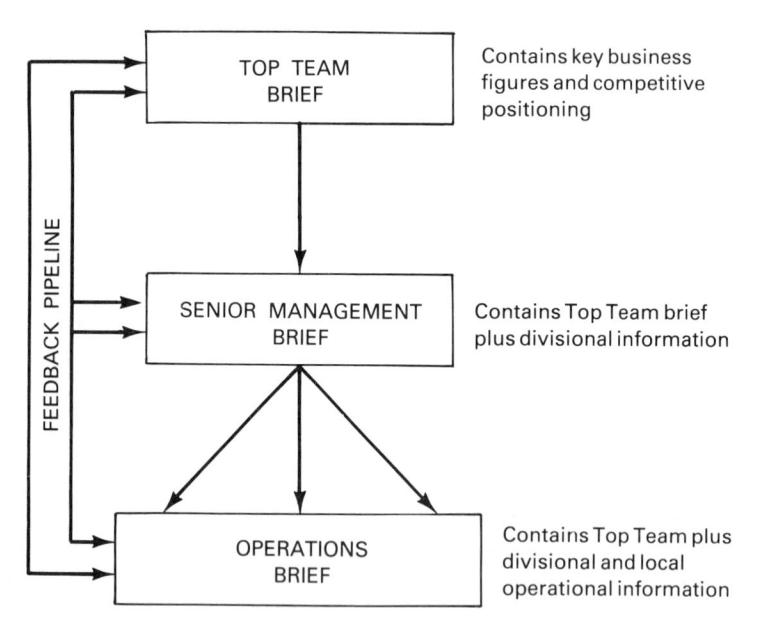

Figure 4.8 Cascade system.

Diagram: Top Team Brief → Senior Management Brief → Operations Brief, with a Feedback Pipeline running back up.
- Top Team Brief: Contains key business figures and competitive positioning
- Senior Management Brief: Contains Top Team brief plus divisional information
- Operations Brief: Contains Top Team plus divisional and local operational information

value if they contribute to the competitive requirements already identified.

It may be necessary to critically examine a few assumed truths in order to achieve the right internal measures, or at least to look critically at the relevance of certain traditional values. For example, there is little point in measuring 'Standard Hours' or efficiency of manufacturing, if the delivery performance to the customer is only 50%! In many cases delivery performance line by line to the customer is not measured at all. By completing a full review of measures internally to support the competitive requirements, many bad and useless practices can be eliminated once and for all.

It is important to ensure all people recognize the key competitive measures and are then encouraged to establish their own internal measures. This can be done by management heading the brainstorm and allowing consensus on the key measures to be established. This procedure takes more time than the typical method of 'management imposed' measures, but is well worth

FULL REVIEW OF MEASURES

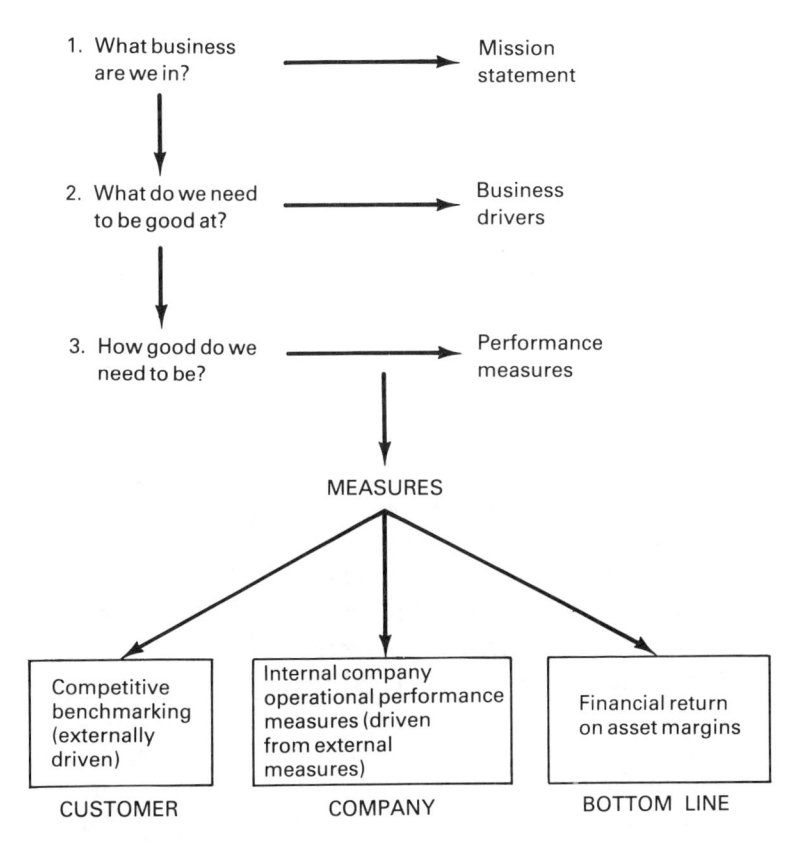

```
1. What business            ─────►    Mission
   are we in?                         statement
   │
   ▼
2. What do we need          ─────►    Business
   to be good at?                     drivers
   │
   ▼
3. How good do we           ─────►    Performance
   need to be?                        measures
                                          │
                                          ▼
                        MEASURES
              ┌──────────────┼──────────────┐
              ▼              ▼              ▼
       Competitive     Internal company   Financial return
       benchmarking    operational        on asset margins
       (externally     performance
       driven)         measures (driven
                       from external
                       measures)
       CUSTOMER        COMPANY            BOTTOM LINE
```

Figure 4.9 Spenley business management process.

the effort. The reason for this is two-fold. First, by involving the people who are responsible for achieving the measures, it is certain that the reason for these particular measures being chosen are understood. Second, the commitment of those people to achieving and beating the measures will be there. In this way, using this methodology for establishing measures against the competitive requirement, it is possible to ensure:

1. Commitment to business objectives from all people.
2. Everyone understands the business requirements and their own measurable contribution.

This process is shown in diagramatic form as Figure 4.9 The Spenley Business Management Process.

CHAPTER FIVE

TQM Structure and top-down requirements

TOP TEAM PLANNING AND STRUCTURE

Having reached the point where the senior management team and executives understand what TQM is, and how it can be used as the management methodology to achieve the required business benefits, there is a requirement to plan implementation. The first requirement is to form a Top Team to plan and control the implementation of TQM throughout the company. The temptation for executives is to 'appoint' a TQM 'implementation team' comprising fairly senior people in the organization, but not including the CEO and directorate. This is a mistake. If the CEO and directorate do not take full responsibility for TQM implementation by forming the Top Team themselves, then two problems will occur.

The first is that because the directorate are not 'doing' they will not fully learn the TQM principles and will not therefore practice them. This will immediately create a barrier between the directorate and the 'implementation team'. There will be a language barrier and therefore a barrier to successful implementation.

The second problem is that everyone in organizations makes judgements on what people do and not what they say. TQM is a people methodology, all people including the directorate, and if the directorate put themselves above this principle by not getting directly involved in TQM, it will fail. The respect will not be earned and it will be impossible to gain the hearts and minds of the people in the organization.

The requirement is to lead by example and the first step in achieving this is to ensure that all the directorate, including the CEO, are active members of the Top Team, planning and controlling the implementation of TQM top-down throughout the organization. The members of the Top Team should comprise the people who are responsible for leading the company.

Top Team selection

Large companies
Large companies have an Executive Board comprising the CEO Group Directorate such as Finance and Personnel, Sales, Marketing and Operational Directors. The Directors in Sales, Marketing and Operations very often have their own directorate. The structure may well look like Figure 5.1.

The group of people, in Figure 5.1, form the first Top Team in the company and have a responsibility to develop the TQM plan which is the plan across the total company. The implementation planning contained in the Chapters 5–13 relate to this group just as importantly, if not even more so, as for all other Top Teams throughout the organization.

The requirement is to develop a Total Plan for the company which can then be taken down the organization by each of the Directors responsible for Sales, Marketing, Operations, Manufacturing and so on. In this case, each of the Directors will form a Top Team of his own to plan and control the implementation locally of TQM through individual plans.

The first Top Team will then form a focal point for the total implementation plan which will ensure co-ordination of planning across the company. This requirement is of paramount importance since all the big problems in an organization are multi-disciplined and cut across functions. For this reason it is advisable to start the implementation across the company at the same time. Again, because the first Top Team is controlling the

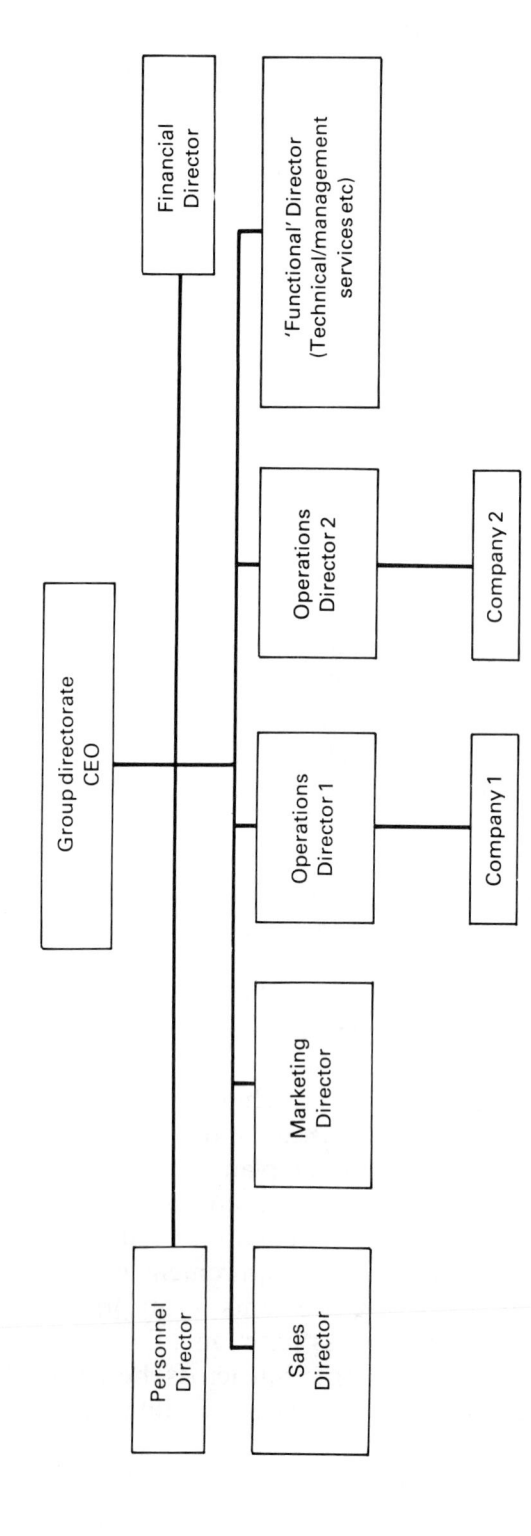

Figure 5.1 Large company structure.

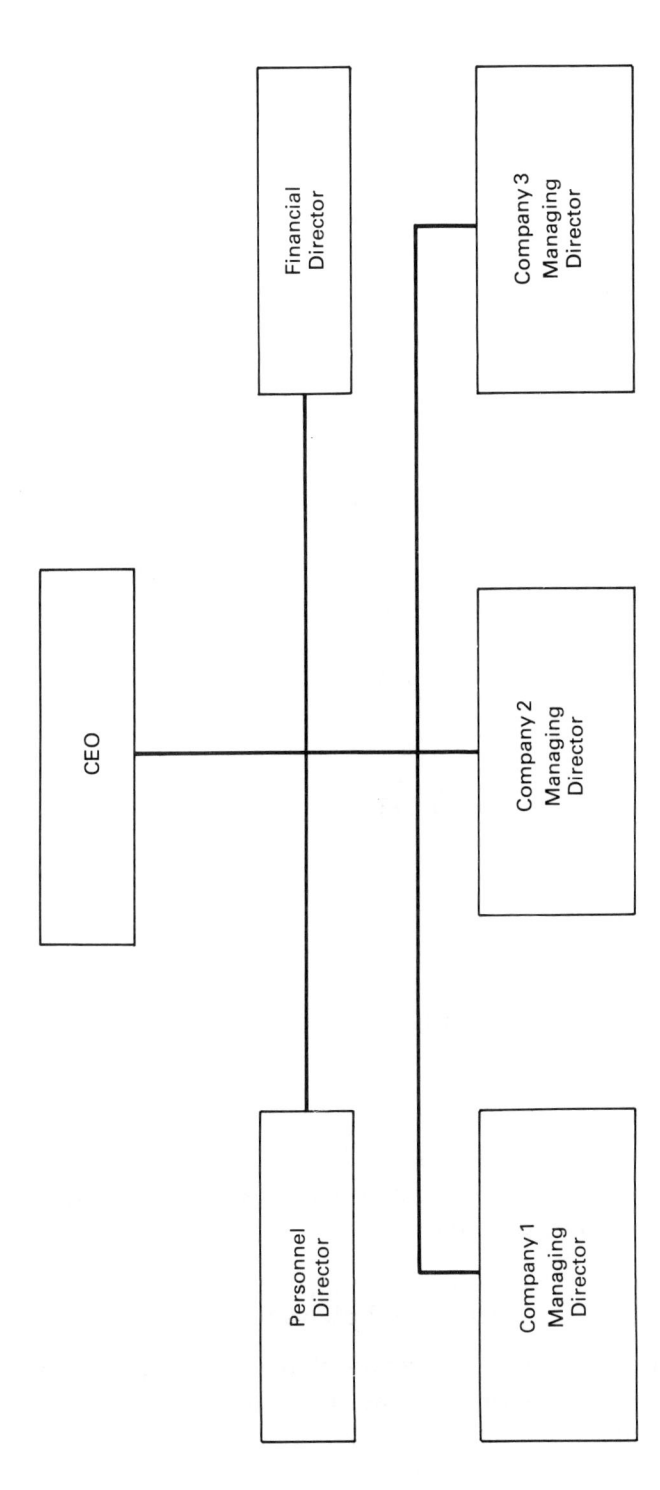

Figure 5.2 Conglomerate structure.

planning and implementation, it is possible to control and coordinate this work successfully.

Conglomerates
The same strategy of top-down implementation relates to the massive conglomerate-type companies. The only difference is that the structure is more likely to look like Figure 5.2.

Each of the companies will have their own structure comprising an organization similar to that described for large companies. In this case there needs to be a total plan for the conglomerates which is then top-down implemented through the companies by each 'Top Team'.

Small/medium-sized companies
The structure may look like Figure 5.3.

In this case there will be only one Top Team and one plan for the implementation of TQM in the organization.

TOP TEAM PLANNING

The above is a guideline to successful implementation. It is the first job of the CEO and his Top Team to determine the Top Team structure needed for the organization – whether it is a huge conglomerate, or a small company of 50 people. The problem is more difficult to solve the larger the organization but the principles remain the same.

TQM IS TOP-DOWN LED AND TOP-DOWN IMPLEMENTED

In every case the first Top Team has to get its act together and pull together a plan for TQM before imposing any actions on the people through the organization.

Structured planning
The Top Team need to understand that TQM implementation is a process and not a programme. It is a process of continuous improvement which requires careful planning, monitoring and

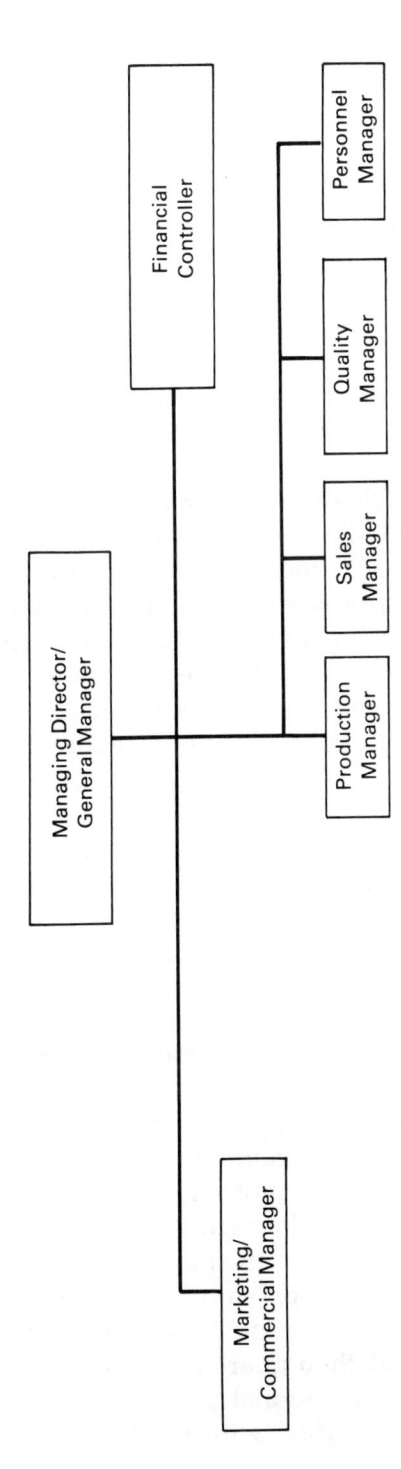

Figure 5.3 Small/medium-sized company structure.

control. It follows, therefore, that sufficient importance must be attached to TQM to warrant a specific Top Team meeting to be held regularly 'for evermore'. This is to say that just as the financial figures are reviewed, say monthly, and actions reviewed or taken to ensure requirements are met, then the TQM Continuous Improvement Process Plan is approached with the same importance. TQM or the Process of Continuous Improvement, is fundamental to the achievement of the financial requirement that the business is judged on by the shareholders.

It will not be possible to succeed with the implementation of TQM if it is seen as a 'bolt-on extra', and 'fitted in' to the monthly financial review or board meeting. This approach is indicative of an uncommitted approach to TQM implementation and will certainly ensure the failure of the continuous improvement process. The requirement is to allocate time to a TQM meeting regularly and with primary importance attached to the meeting to ensure attendance. Normally this meeting should be held monthly and should last for a minimum of 2 hours and a maximum of 3 hours.

The first commitment given to TQM implementation is to allocate the time and commit attendance to this meeting. This is not an easy task to achieve in many companies where Top Team members have crowded diaries and very little time for planning – all the time is spent 'running the business' – which is precisely why these Top Teams need to implement TQM.

The first step in improving the way the business is run is to take TQM seriously and commit to structured planning meetings. It is essential for the success of TQM that it is planned and integrated into the management requirements. The success of every activity depends on thorough planning and total commitment and the first requirement of top management is to recognize this fact and allocate the planning time accordingly.

Typically an Executive Top Team in a conglomerate responsible for many operations should meet initially monthly to develop the plan, and then quarterly to review progress and help co-ordinate the operational plans. The operational Top Teams should meet monthly, with the Directors of the operations also being members of the executive Top Team, and providing good two-way communications.

In smaller companies the Top Team need to meet monthly, although in all cases it is necessary to spend more time in the initial stages to develop the plan – typically meeting every two weeks until an agreed plan is developed. From that stage, monthly meetings are the requirement.

The elements of the plan

The planning for TQM is the responsibility of the Top Team. This team is accountable for developing, monitoring and controlling TQM implementation. The methodology is activity-based, not 'homework-marking'. It is essential for the Top Team to be seen to be leading the implementation – this means by doing not talking! When each member of the Top Team takes accountability for the successful implementation of each element of the TQM plan, there is a very good chance that the TQM implementation will be successful. Where the Top Team does not take accountability there is no chance of success.

The elements of the TQM plan are detailed in Chapters 7–12 and will act as a guide to those Top Team members who are accountable for one of the TQM implementation elements.

Top Team dynamics

Each member of the Top Team is allocated responsibility for an element and reports back to the Top Team meeting on proposed policies and activities that need to be taken into account to ensure success. The team then need to discuss the points for and against the proposal and together agree the plan. In this way all members of the Top Team are committed to the plan and will all say and do the same thing with their people in the organization.

It is important to understand that the member of the Top Team responsible for an element of the plan is there to advise the other Top Team members. It is up to the whole team to ensure the implementation of the plan, together. There are only two elements where it is necessary to fix the accountability – for all the other elements it is best policy to ask for volunteers for element accountability.

The two elements which are not voluntary are Quality Policy and Cost of Quality.

Quality Policy
This accountability for this element needs to lie with the Chief Executive or top manager in the Top Team. The Quality Policy is not just a set of words, it is a set of values by which TQM implementation will be successful. This must come from the top of the organization.

Cost of Quality
The Financial Director or the Financial Controller needs to take accountability for this element. If not, he may feel defensive where someone else in the Top Team is talking about the financial measures of the TQM implementation. It is essential for the Financial Director to fully understand the Cost of Quality principles, take responsibilities for the analysis, and for the development and implementation of the on-going Cost of Quality Monitoring Systems. This will ensure full commitment to Cost of Quality and will make financial resourcing for TQM a much simpler and shorter process.

TQM IMPLEMENTATION TEAM ORGANIZATIONAL STRUCTURE

When the Top Team in the organization is meeting to develop the TQM implementation plan, this can be termed the first continuous improvement team.

A structure for TQM implementation and continuous improvement teamwork is required for the organization, as shown in Figure 5.4.

The planning and actions required are defined in Chapters 6–13 as elements in the Top Team implementation plan. This structure must be implemented to ensure that people in the organization are allowed time formally to solve problems. It

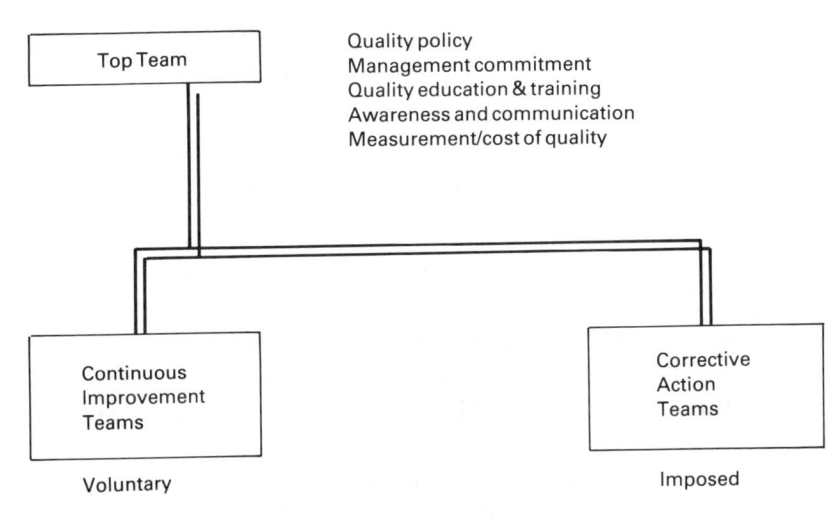

```
┌──────────┐   Quality policy
│ Top Team │   Management commitment
└────┬─────┘   Quality education & training
     │        Awareness and communication
     │        Measurement/cost of quality
     │
  ┌──┴────────────────────┐
  │                       │
┌─┴──────────┐     ┌──────┴─────┐
│ Continuous │     │ Corrective │
│Improvement │     │  Action    │
│  Teams     │     │  Teams     │
└────────────┘     └────────────┘
  Voluntary            Imposed
```

Figure 5.4 TQM structure.

means time, financial resources and training being provided – which is why these issues are an element of the Top Team planning.

The challenge is to ensure that all the people in the organization are active members of a Quality Improvement team. This is a fundamental requirement of the TQM Continuous Improvement Process and when this is achieved there will be a culture of continuous improvement in the organization. It is this structure which stops TQM implementation 'running out of steam' after the initial burst of activity and training – a problem all too common for many Western companies.

The successful Japanese companies are characterized by almost 100% involvement in Quality Improvement Teams. This is not achieved without commitment, understanding and involvement from the Top Team. It is not easy to obtain 100% involvement, but it is a requirement. Too often, Western companies will fail to recognize the importance of this Quality Improvement Team structure. A typical quote is 'we can't allow people to have an hour a week off the job!' Why not? What could be more important than meeting to continuously improve the way the business is run – and when 100% of the people in the organization, including the Top Team, are all doing this – what a competitive advantage this is!

Management commitment

This could more aptly be named 'leading by example'. It is a fundamental requirement that management lead by example in the Quality Improvement Process. This means fully understanding the Quality principles, and most important of all, practising them. Once this requirement is accepted, it is necessary to think through the actions that need to be taken to ensure success.

As already explained, the commitment to a TQM Planning meeting must be made and adhered to. It is then up to that member of the Top Team who has the responsibility for the management commitment element to advise the rest of the team on the actions they must all take. The following ideas promote a foundation to work on:

1. **Commitment to quality – first and always** – must be demonstrated. The requirement is for management to provide a focus on quality, by always putting quality first. For example, on all staff meetings, make sure quality is placed the first item on the agenda throughout the organization. A full review of measures in the organization needs to be carried out to ensure that quality is understood and is being measured correctly.
2. **Education and Training** is required for all the people in the organization to enable everyone to practise continuous improvement.
3. **Communication channels** must be improved to ensure full awareness of the company position, and the effect of the TQM Continuous Improvement Process.
4. **A Quality Improvement team** structure must be put in place starting with the Top Team and developing 100% involvement of the people in the organization through Continuous Improvement teams, and Corrective Action teams.
5. **Problem solving methods and systems** need to be estab-

lished to ensure that errors are completely removed, and never allowed to return. The tools and techniques explained in Part Three will be useful here.
6. **Recognition and reward** is a requirement to ensure 'Quality Champions' in the organization are properly recognized, and their commitment to quality re-inforced.
7. **A Cost of Quality system** has to be established to financially monitor the success of the TQM Continuous Improved Process, and to allow a priority for Corrective Action Plans to be carried out.

Along with the Quality Policy these are the elements of the Top Team TQM Implementation Plan.

It requires a continuous commitment to this TQM implementation plan by the Top Team – not in the initial stages where there is a lot of work required to develop a plan, but also a commitment when some success has been achieved and there is a tendency to settle back and think the job has been completed. In the TQM Continuous Improvement Process, there is no end, therefore there is no end to the Top Team meeting schedule.

This 'planning, monitoring and action' methodology has to be recognized as the key to success and management commitment is an absolute requirement to making it happen.

Financial support

Clearly such a major plan involving all the people in the organization cannot succeed if financial support is not forthcoming. Finance will be needed for education and training, equipment, materials and so on, to enable Quality improvements to be made. The first time a well-prepared Quality Improvement Plan is not approved by Management, because of 'lack of funds' the whole TQM Quality Improvement Process will lose credibility. Who would bother spending time to solve a problem when management doesn't provide the financial resource to implement the improvement?

All Quality Improvement plans must be reviewed formally and a positive response from Management given. There must be a commitment and involvement with the Quality Improvement plans, to ensure all Quality Improvements are to the benefit of the business.

Individual commitment

Apart from management commitment to the TQM Quality Improvement Process, there is a need for a Personal Quality Improvement Plan. This applies equally to everyone in the organization, not just management. However, it is necessary for the Top Team to <u>begin</u> the process by each member of the Top Team deciding on one or more activities to which he or she commits to making a continuous improvement. Some examples are included here to give an idea of the type of activities to which individuals can demonstrate a personal commitment to the TQM Continuous Improvement Process:

- Commit to a Policy of never changing the time or venue of a meeting you have called.
- Commit to starting the meeting on time and finishing on time.
- Commit to a policy of correspondence clearance within 24 hours.
- Commit to ensuring your secretary can read your writing so that she can have a commitment to zero errors and you don't then have to check her typing.
- Commit to the GOYA Policy – that is to 'get off your a***' and ensure a daily walkabout amongst your people whenever you are in the office. Also, make sure you don't always speak to the same people all the time!
- Commit to answering the telephone within three rings.

It is important that all the Top Team members start to demonstrate their individual commitment to the TQM Continuous Improvement Process at the same time – otherwise messages will be sent down the organization that only certain members of the Top Team are committed to quality. This must be avoided by Top Team planning and action! Remember that it is much easier to obtain individual commitment from the people that work for

Figure 5.5 Receptionist – three rings.

you if you are leading by example. In other words, 'I'm doing it – why can't you?' If you have any doubt that there is an activity that can be improved, it is a salutory lesson to ask those people that work for you. They will provide some ideas!

CHAPTER SIX

Quality policy

- What is the company's policy on Quality?
- What does the company mean when the word Quality is used?
- Is the company a 'Quality Company'?

These questions must all be addressed by the Top Team and clear unambiguous answers provided for all the people that work in the company. It is the role of the top person in the Top Team, that is the Chief Executive, Managing Director, or General Manager, to think through the above issues and provide a set of guidelines to the Top Team members.

The guidelines need then to be discussed at the first Top Team TQM Planning meeting and a policy and set of values agreed. It is important for the Top Person to think the Quality Policy issues through alone before sharing and brainstorming with the other Top Team members to obtain agreement. In this way, leadership will be coming from the top by doing. It doesn't matter if the words used are not 'slick' or 'media-style', what does matter is that they come from within. This will make communication easier and will ensure respect; everyone will know that the top person, whenever he or she speaks quality, believes in it. This is leading by example, and is absolutely critical to the success of TQM in the organization.

FRAMING A QUALITY POLICY

The Quality Policy needs to be short and succinct; it is a mistake to confuse the policy statement with a set of values which can make the 'Quality Policy' two or three pages long. This will ensure nobody can ever remember it, very few will actually read the words, and the paper will be consigned to the rubbish bin or a filing cabinet.

The Quality Policy needs to be a 'living' policy. It needs to be understood and remembered by everyone; it needs to be on the walls, desks, (and carpets!) of the business; it needs to be signed by everyone in the organization as their personal commitment to Quality. This should be done during the education and training process, not before training. The details of how this process of employee signature of the Quality Policy helps obtain commitment is included in Chapter 9 – Education and Training.

A Policy two or three pages long is not meeting the requirement! The actual words used are obviously the prerogative of the Top Team but there are certain factors that need to be included, which follow directly from the Total Quality Management Principles detailed in Chapter 3.

The Policy must underpin the following principles:

- Quality means meeting customer requirements.
- Customers are both external and internal.
- By meeting customer requirements the company will achieve and maintain a competitive edge against the competition.
- Quality means achieving a culture of continuous improvement in all areas of the company.

The Quality principles are all the information that is required to answer the three questions posed at the beginning of this Chapter.

Encompassing these principles into a short succinct form of words called the 'Quality Policy' is easier said than done! However, it is worth the mental effort and time of the top person in the Top Team, and of course the Top Team itself in the TQM planning meeting. To help things along a little, this is the Quality Policy I favour; and which also proves my own Quality Policy.

> TO ACHIEVE AND MAINTAIN A COMPETITIVE EDGE BY MEETING EXTERNAL AND INTERNAL REQUIREMENTS THROUGH THE PROCESS OF CONTINUOUS IMPROVEMENTS

Figure 6.1 The Spenley quality policy.

Quality Policy – set of values

Having established the Quality Policy, there needs to be a set of values to support the achievement of the policy. The mechanism for achieving these values is to brainstorm during the TQM Top Team planning meeting all the requirements needed to ensure that the Quality Policy can be met. It is important to go through this mechanism as it will get out, on the table, all the barriers to successful implementation. For example:

- Is Quality first against output?
- Is the company customer-orientated? Or is it being run for the employees at the expense of the customer?
- Is there a Process of Continuous Improvement?
- Is the company 'fix-it' orientated? Are root cause problems ignored?

It is an exercise in total honesty where there is a recognition that the TQM process is not going to be easy; it will take time, planning, effort and courage. It stops the process of management self-delusion setting in, while the temptation is to start plastering the walls with the newly-formed Quality Policy!

Total Quality

This is a typical shopping list of the Quality Policy values that need to be achieved in the organization:

- Achieving global competitive advantage
- Process of continuous improvement
- Eliminating waste in the organization
- Involves everyone
- Requires a cultural change; a change in attitude to continuous improvement

- Improves customer service and satisfaction
- Ensures everyone understands their role in the business and what is needed to achieve company objectives
- Everyone understands the internal customer/supplier chain
- Everyone has agreed measures between customer and supplier
- Ensures total teamwork
- Breaks down functional barriers
- Eliminate problem once and for all

The list is only a small number of elements that are brainstormed in the first Top Team planning meeting.

TQM – QUALITY OF CUSTOMER SERVICE

It is important at this stage to fully understand the total breadth across the company. In the Quality Policy the key word is 'customer'. In the set of values that are established to support the Quality Policy, it is necessary to clearly state that it is applicable right across the organization.

The diagram in Figure 6.2 is designed to clearly show the definition of Quality across all operations and functions of the company. This can be broken down into the Quality of all the

QUALITY OF PRODUCT   QUALITY OF SALES

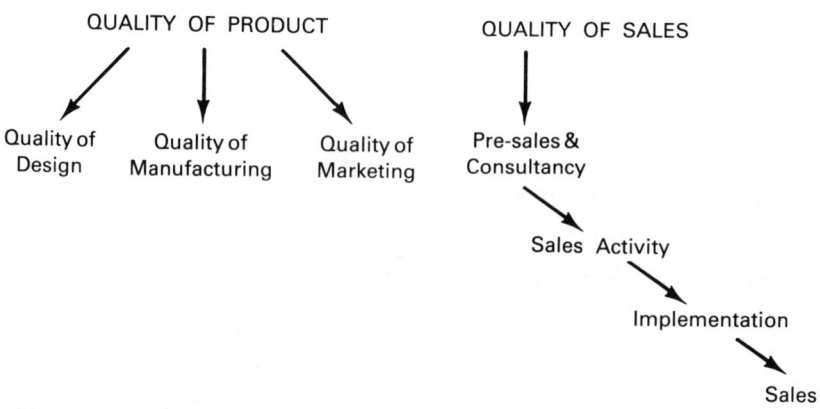

Quality of   Quality of   Quality of   Pre-sales &
Design   Manufacturing   Marketing   Consultancy
                                                  ↓
                                             Sales Activity
                                                  ↓
                                             Implementation
                                                  ↓
                                                 Sales

Figure 6.2 Quality of service to the customer.

functions that ultimately provide the customer service, whether this is a product, a hotel booking, a restaurant meal, an airline reservation or whatever. In other words, the Quality of service offered to the customer is dependant on <u>everyone</u> in the organization, not just those who have direct dealings with the customer.

This understanding is one of the KEY VALUES of the Quality Policy.

CHAPTER SEVEN

Measurement

INDIVIDUAL MEASUREMENT

The requirement is that every person in the organization gets used to a 'measurement culture' and finds a way of measuring his or her activities.

To demonstrate this individual commitment to continuous improvement it is necessary to draw up and maintain a 'visible' measure of progress. The best way of doing this is to use a simple measurement chart which is updated by the individual each day. It is important not to ask the Secretary to update the chart – this is defeating the object!

The chart should then be displayed in a prominent position where the individual's commitment to quality improvement can be publicly viewed. For example outside the manager's office, not inside. Not only does this show commitment but it also has the effect of ensuring the manager really does make efforts to improve, since his or her failures are publicly on view.

Experience of this approach has shown that people respect the manager for firstly accepting that he or she isn't perfect, and are then prepared to follow the example set, whereby failure is not hidden, and there is a determination to improve. This is strong and positive leadership, and provides the atmosphere which everyone else in the organization will follow suit and agree to a Personal Quality Improvement Measure, again which is fully visible.

The process of adopting an individual measure and charting

progress, leads to the establishment of a 'measurement and improvement culture' in the organization.

AGREED BUSINESS MEASURES

This measurement culture is understood and practised by everyone in the organization, and allows the use of business measures in all areas of the company.

Business measures are not the individual measures discussed in the last section of this Chapter – these are the hundreds, even thousands of measures which are taken day-in, day-out by the organization to ensure customer requirements are met every time.

These measures, as detailed in Chapter 4, are the result of a top-down review, ensuring the company is focussing on external customer requirements which provide a competitive edge to the company. For example, the requirement to deliver 100% on time, the product or service that the customer expects. These external customer measures then drive a whole series of internal customer measures throughout the organization. The TQM methodology for defining the correct measures is based on communication and involvement.

Communication

As detailed in Chapter 4, it is necessary to ensure everyone in the organization is aware of the key external customer measures the company is measuring, and why they are important. In other words 'if we do this we will achieve and maintain a competitive edge in the marketplace'. These measures then need to be fully visible to everyone in the organization as everyone should know how the company is doing – they are all part of the company after all!

There are methods for achieving this:

- Key external customer measures should be displayed throughout the company, on simple measurement charts,

showing monthly, weekly or even daily results, dependent on the type of business.
- If there is a Network Information System, the key measures should be available on computer terminals available to everyone.
- All staff meetings must include an update on company performance.

There is sometimes concern that the total visibility of failure which measurement charts obviously show can be detrimental to customers or potential customers visiting the company. This concern needs to be discussed in the Top Team meeting and the individual circumstances of the company and its customer base taken into account. However, I have never known any customer, or potential customer, be anything but impressed with the total commitment to quality improvement which full visibility of measures demonstrates.

Involvement

The ability to ensure that the internal customer measures in the organization fully support and contribute to the external customer measures is dependent on the involvement of all people. This begins, as discussed, with the understanding and full visibility of the external measures required.

The next stage is to define the Divisional, Sectional or Departmental measures needed. This should be done by the Top Team who have the responsibility to cascade down the external measures and then involve the people below them in the organization in the definition of the internal measures required. This, in time, should be cascaded down lower into the organization until a full set of Agreed Measures is obtained.

The Measurement Top Team member has the responsibility for planning this process on behalf of the organization, and co-ordinating the measures.

The key to success is to obtain agreement between the internal customer and supplier in all cases. This is the application of the TQM principles detailed in Chapter 3, using the internal

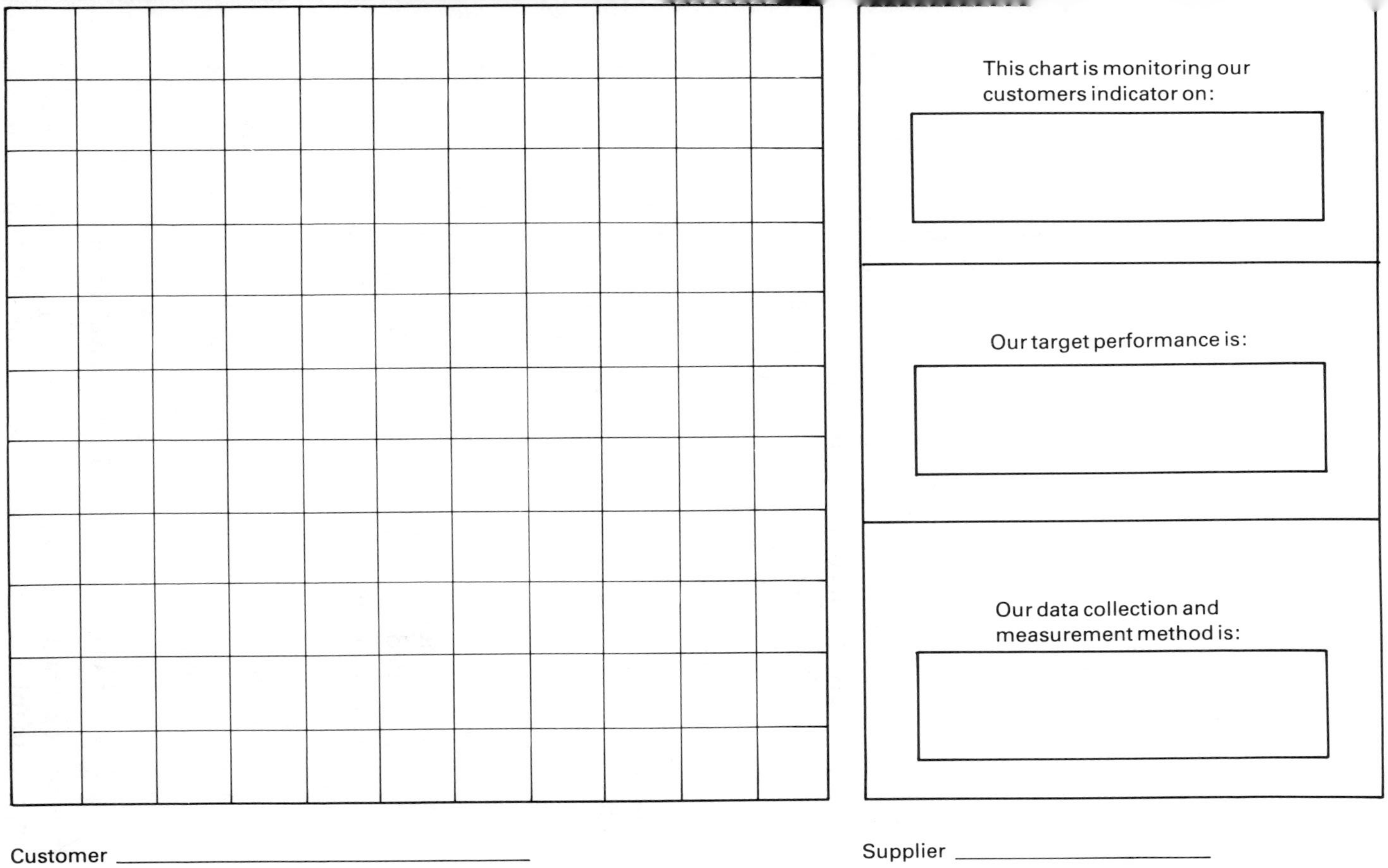

This chart is monitoring our customers indicator on:

Our target performance is:

Our data collection and measurement method is:

Customer _____   Supplier _____

Figure 7.1 Team indicator chart.

customer/supplier principle, and defining agreed requirements at all times. The customer/supplier relationship will be between division at one level, between departments at another level, between the sections at another level, and ultimately of course between individuals.

At all times requirements need to be agreed between the customer and supplier, and measurement charts should be established. It is a good idea to have a section on the measurement chart which identifies who the customer is, who is the supplier, and to have a signature from each to demonstrate agreement to the measure. A typical chart layout is shown in Figure 7.1. This can be done for divisions, sections, departments, and of course individuals and shows that the TQM principles have been correctly applied.

The total involvement of everyone in the organization in the measurement cascade, ensures that the people doing the job can measure their own work, and because of the involvement and commitment are able to correct problems when they occur, rather than wait for some 'specialist' to correct the problem. Or even worse 'throw the problem up to management' to solve. This measurement culture will allow up to 90% of problems to be solved when they occur between the internal customer and supplier.

However, 10% of problems will be out of the scope and influence of the people doing the job; these problems will require some management support and effort to resolve, possibly involving skilled problem solving techniques, like Taguchi, DOE (Design of Experiments), or SPC (Statistical Process Control).

It is important to remember that simple measurement methods applied with commitment, intelligence, and involvement of all people will solve 90% of the problems in an organization, continuously.

Cost of Total Quality – measurement

It is necessary to measure the effect of the TQM Quality Improvement Process in the organization in financial terms.

AGREED BUSINESS MEASURES

Applying the Cost of Total Quality System enables this, by providing a financial standard.

As detailed in Chapter 3

Cost of Total Quality = Cost of Conformance +
Cost of Non-conformance

Cost of Conformance is the cost of investing to ensure activities are achieved to the agreed requirement and problems prevented from occurring.

Cost of Non-conformance is the cost incurred by failing to achieve activities to the agreed requirement.

The Cost of Conformance should be measured initially to determine the total cost of investment in the TQM Quality Improvement Process. There will be an investment required in terms of people's time, the facilities required, and systems and equipment to enable people to improve the way they run the business.

TQM has to be budgeted for and the following items identified and established as investment costs. In other words, the Cost of Conformance Costs should be viewed as 'investment capital', not as a 'consumable cost'.

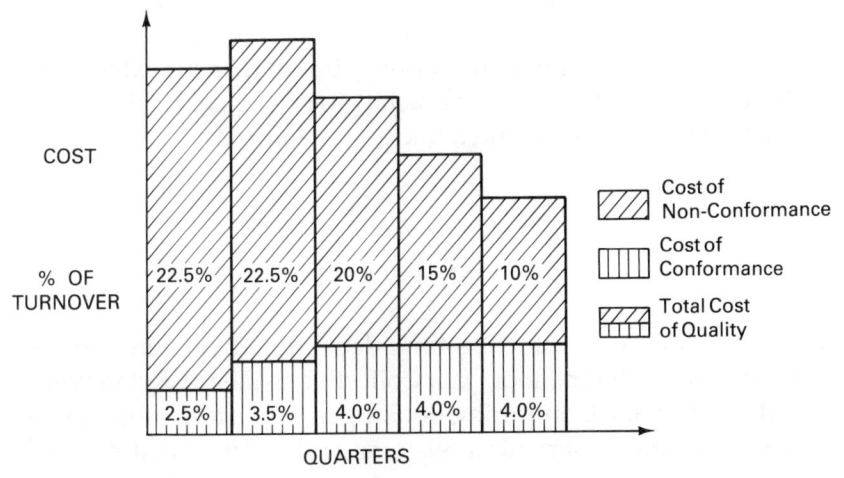

Figure 7.2 Typical cost of quality trends.

COC – people's time (100% of employees)
Education and training time : 10 days/annum
Formal problem solving time: 1 hour/week

This can easily be converted into a financial figure based on this hourly rate for employees, and so give a message of the financial commitment in people's time that is required. Remember it may take up to two years or more to get 100% of people into improvement teams – this doesn't happen overnight!

When this commitment to people's time is measured financially it may cause some concern; remember this is an investment that will be returned hundreds of times over.

COC – materials costs
> Specialist support costs
> Books
> Conferences

These costs are necessary to ensure State-of-the-Art knowledge in TQM, and may include specialist consultancy and training skills, videos and so on.

COC – facilities
The training facilities to enable formal education, and to accommodate improvement team meetings need to be established as a permanent requirement. The exact requirements are detailed in Chapter 9 on Education and Training, but may incur extra costs if there is not a suitable training facility in existence. Again, these costs may be significant and a budget is required.

SYSTEMS AND EQUIPMENT

Improved methods of collecting data and displaying information, such as Shop Floor Data Collection Systems, Retail Point of Sale Terminals, Computing Booking Systems for Hotel Reservations, Airline Reservation Systems and so on, must be considered.

It is not recommended that the cost of equipment/systems is included in the Cost of Conformance, as this expenditure is always viewed individually with a financial business case. However, it is important to understand that as people become more aware of what can be done to improve efficiency and productivity, more requests for systems and equipment improvements will be made than before, and management need to be aware, be able to respond and control this expectation.

It is not possible to successfully obtain the benefits of TQM, without being prepared to invest because

> Investment in COC (Cost of Conformance) is a pre-requisite to Reduction in CONC (Cost of Non-Conformance).

Figure 7.2 shows this relationship. There should be no surprises!

The Cost of Non-Conformance is the cost incurred by failing to achieve activities to the agreed requirements. The implementation plan for ensuring education of CONC must contain the following elements:

- A Cost of Quality Analysis (CONC)
- A Company Cost of Quality Model (CONC)
- A Full Cause and Effect Analysis

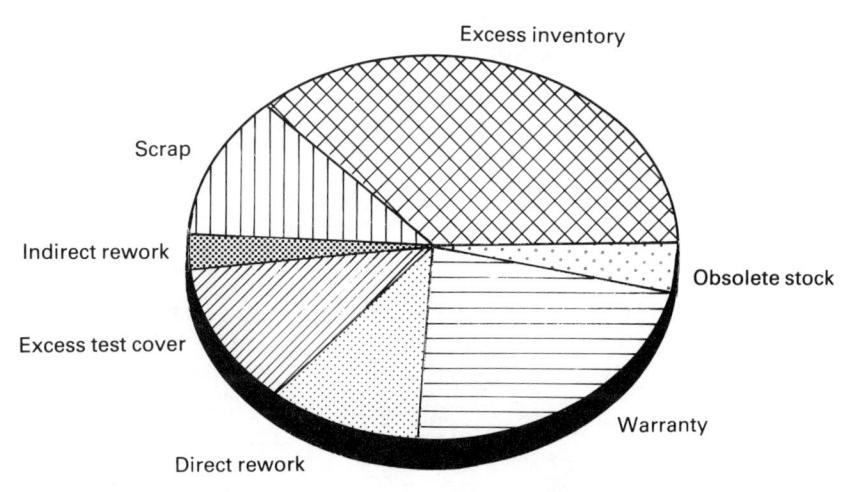

Figure 7.3 Quality costs in manufacturing activities.

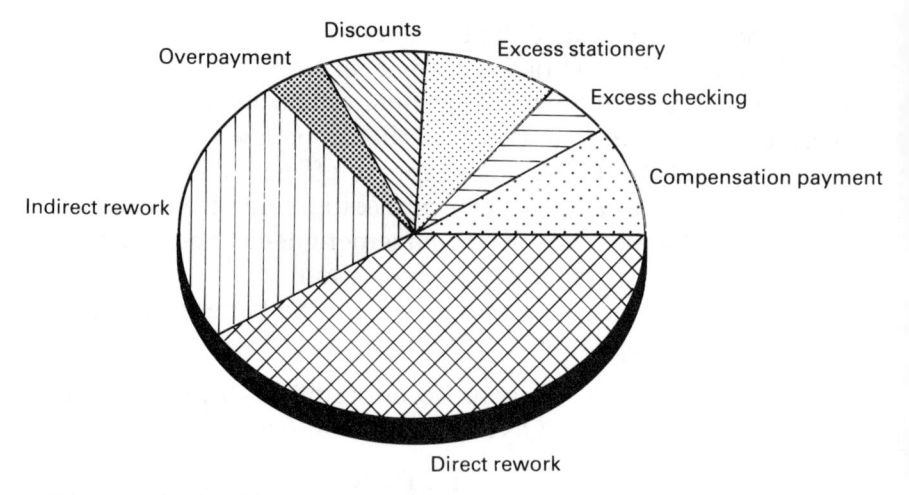

Figure 7.4 Quality costs in service activities.

- A Cost-Prioritized Corrective Action Plan
- Cost of Quality and Tools and Techniques Education
- Formula of Corrective Action Teams to reduce the non-conformance costs.

Cost of quality analysis
Typical cost of quality analyses for manufacturing and service activities are shown in Figures 7.3 and 7.4.

CHAPTER EIGHT

Quality improvement teams

Implementing a Quality improvement team culture into the organization is a key factor in ensuring the TQM Quality Improvement Process does not tail off after the initial enthusiasm. This was discussed in Chapter 5, where the improvement team structure was outlined. The structure is simple to understand but difficult to implement successfully.

One of the biggest problems in the TQM implementation process in the West is keeping enthusiasm and commitment going after the initial Cost of Quality work has been completed. This is because the Quality improvement team requirements are not fully understood at Top Team level. Too often, Quality improvement teams and Quality circles are seen as 'nice to have' but not essential.

It is important to understand that the successful implementation of Quality improvement teams is an absolute essential to the achievement of a continuous improvement culture. The requirement is to obtain 100% employee involvement in improvement teams. When this is completed, 100% of the people are actively working on Quality improvement.

This is the key competitive edge in any organization, and is the secret of success for Japanese companies. Although the Japanese methods for achieving TQM have been studied in detail for many years, this 100% Quality improvement team involvement is always admired but often put down to the 'Japanese culture'. In other words, it is 'impossible to achieve in a Western culture'. This type of ignorance is what will

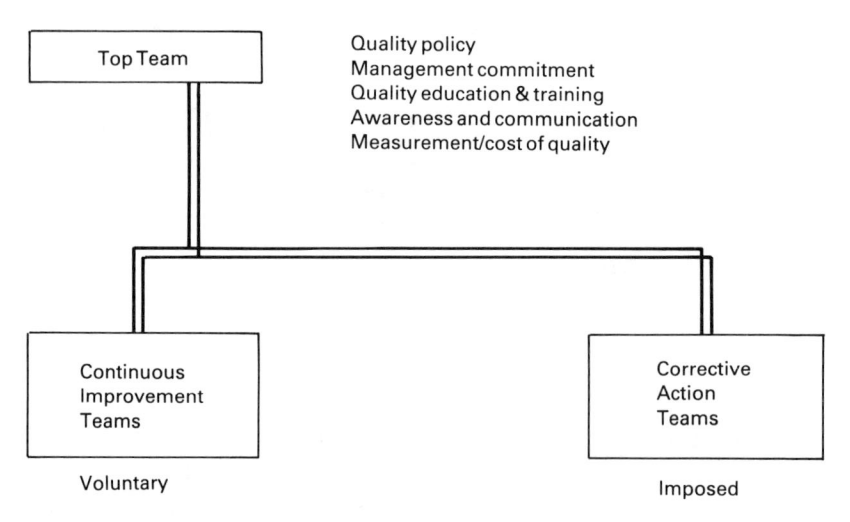

```
                              Quality policy
       ┌──────────┐           Management commitment
       │ Top Team │           Quality education & training
       └──────────┘           Awareness and communication
                              Measurement/cost of quality

   ┌──────────────┐                      ┌──────────────┐
   │ Continuous   │                      │ Corrective   │
   │ Improvement  │                      │ Action       │
   │ Teams        │                      │ Teams        │
   └──────────────┘                      └──────────────┘
     Voluntary                              Imposed
```

Figure 8.1 Quality Improvement Team structure.

keep Western companies lagging behind the Japanese. Why shouldn't it be possible to achieve 100% employee involvement in the Quality improvement process? There is no good reason. The implementation of the structure detailed in this book will provide the foundation, whereby, over a period of time, 100% employee involvement can be achieved and maintained.

PUTTING THE STRUCTURE IN PLACE

The Top Team need to have a member who is responsible for Quality improvement teams. It is his or her job to define the policies, plans and actions which need to be taken to obtain 100% involvement. These plans then need to be agreed at Top Team level, and of course implemented by all members of the Top Team.

Policy

1. To obtain 100% employee involvement in Quality improvement teams.

2. To allow improvement teams the time, during working hours, to meet formally. This should be for one hour maximum per week, typically.
3. To ensure 100% of people are educated in problem solving techniques.
4. To ensure 100% of people understand and practise good meetings discipline such that all improvement team meetings are productive, and not just 'whingeing sessions'.

Planning
The Top Team who is planning and maintaining the Quality improvement process is the first Quality improvement team to be formed. This is an important structure to make, and an important point of understanding for all members of the Top Team. They need to feel part of the TQM team culture and provide a role model for the rest of the organization.

Figure 8.2 Management commitment.

Structure

There are two types of improvement team:

- Imposed : Corrective action teams
- Voluntary: Continuous improvement teams

The first teams to be established in the TQM improvement process are the corrective action teams. As detailed in the previous Chapter, it is necessary to identify areas for improvement, prioritized financially, and obtain profitable benefit quickly. By following the Cost of Quality implementation planning, the corrective action team structure is achieved, in the early stages of TQM implementation planning.

Cost of Quality, therefore, is the vehicle for driving corrective action teams. The nature of corrective action teams is transitory, they are formed in order to solve a particular problem and when that is done they disband. It is the task or project style of team working, often under pressure. They are a necessary part of the Quality improvement team structure, and will provide major benefits to the organization.

Continuous improvement teams, on the other hand, are groups of people who meet together voluntarily to improve Quality. They may come from the same work area, or the same work function; for example a group of Secretaries. There are no set rules as to who should be part of a continuous improvement team. It may include people from Design, Marketing, Sales, Manufacturing and Finance, who may be meeting to continuously improve the process of product introduction, sales order processing, customer service etc. As already stated, the Top Team are meeting to ensure the process of continuous improvement across the whole organization is successfully established and maintained.

It must be understood that because of this, it follows that everyone in the organization can be a member of a continuous improvement team. This includes Managers, Project Leaders, Clerks, Sales Executives, Marketing Managers, Accountants, Engineers, Directors, and Secretaries. The teams may be Departmental, Inter-departmental, Inter-factory or Inter-organization etc. In many successful companies continuous improvement teams are established between the company and its customers, which ensures the rapid formation of a business process culture between customer and supplier, and a continuous improvement in customer satisfaction.

MANAGEMENT ROLE IN CONTINUOUS IMPROVEMENT TEAMS

Continuous improvement teams cannot be successful if management don't think it applies to them. This has traditionally been the problem with Quality circles which is another name for continuous improvement teams. In many cases management saw Quality circles as something for the workforce only, 'it doesn't apply to me'. This led to a lack of understanding of what the Quality circles were there for, what they did, and consequently a cynical view of their contribution to the business at work. There would be many attempts by middle management to stop Quality circles meeting, and at best a resigned tolerance of their existence.

This attitude is basically ignorant, not to mince words! The management must understand they need to improve as well as the people working for them, and therefore provide a role model, an example for their people. This is best done by being involved in a continuous improvement team themselves. The Top Team can claim to be a continuous improvement team. One of the tasks of the Top Team is to ensure that their management understand the improvement team policy, and learn how to operate a successful continuous improvement team. This will include the learning and application of problem solving techniques and of good meetings discipline.

When management are aware of how continuous improvement teams work by being involved, they are then in a position to encourage their people to follow suit. It follows that continuous improvement teams take longer to establish than corrective action teams, in the TQM improvement process. As long as this is understood by the Top Team, there is an excellent chance that continuous improvement teams will become a part of the company culture.

The manager's role in a continuous improvement team formed by members of his staff, has to be that of a 'respected helper'. In other words, the manager needs to be there to help guide the improvement team forward and to unblock problems that they come up against. It is not necessary to attend every meeting, but it is necessary to show interest and commitment to the team. It is also important to be fully aware of the project or projects that the continuous improvement team work on. This is to ensure that the project is going to provide benefits and not be a 'waste of time and effort'. In other words be careful to avoid projects that are irrelevant, unwieldy, or too far out of the scope of the improvement team. If this happens, the team will not be successful and there will be a reluctance for those people to continue.

Choosing projects

When a continuous improvement team meet for the first time, the requirement is to 'brainstorm' problems. This is the formal method of each person in turn thinking up of problems that affect he or she doing his or her job to requirements. It is not unusual to obtain as many as 50 problem areas in a ten-minute brainstorm.

These problems are then analysed to see how they fall into three catagories, as shown in Figure 8.3

- T – 'Totally' under the group control, that is to say problems which can be solved by the group themselves with no assistance.
- P – 'Partially' under group control, but which need specialist help to resolve, either from the manager, or other departments.
- N – 'Not' under control at all, problems which are entirely out of the scope of the group and which should be referred to the Top Team.

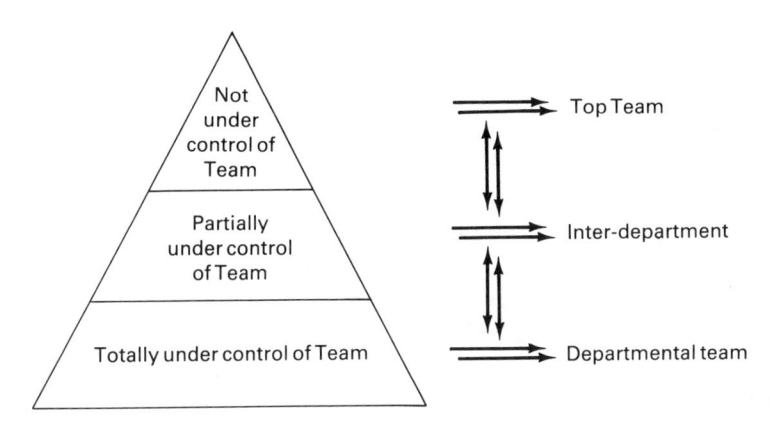

Figure 8.3 Problem solving structure for improvement teams.

The 'T' problems are usually solved by the group within a short time, provide quick benefits, and a feeling that the team is working.

The 'P' problems need guidance from management to ensure that the basis on which the problems should be chosen to solve first is right. These type of problems are tougher to solve than the 'T' problems, and need to be discussed with the manager to ensure the project chosen is valid and supported. These type of projects may take up to 6 months to solve. It is usual for continuous improvement teams to successfully complete two projects every year.

The 'N' problems need to be reviewed by the group with managers to ascertain whether a corrective action team should be formed which for example, would include people from Marketing, Design, Sales, or even from the supplier or customer.

Continuous Improvement Teams have great value in not only improving their own work methods, but also identifying problems which need to be addressed by the company on a larger scale. This is a good example of how continuous improvement teams and corrective action teams can work together.

Review of projects

It is important for the Top Team to establish a structure whereby all the continuous improvement team projects are formally received. This is necessary to ensure projects are valued, good work is recognized, and the necessary resources are planned, budgeted for and implemented.

The first request is for all members of the Top Team to take responsibilities for helping teams get started, and keep going, in their department – in other words to feel ownership. It is the Management's responsibility to educate their people so that everyone knows what a continuous improvement team is, how it works and what the benefits are to the individual and to the company. This is part of the education and training process, and it is vital that it is the manager who gets these messages across, and provides the route by which people volunteer to become members of a continuous improvement team.

It follows that this step should not be taken until the Top Team in a company is fully competent as a continuous improvement team itself. The culture of the continuous improvement team is then generated top-down throughout the organization. This approach obviously takes time, but is essential for the successful achievement of 100% involvement in the organization, and to on-going continuous improvement.

CHAPTER NINE

Education and training

The education requirement is to ensure that everyone in the organization knows what is required of them, and why. The training requirement is to ensure that everyone is capable of solving the problems that inhibit the achievement of their objectives. It is not sufficient to send people on Problem Solving training courses alone, and think this will cover the TQM requirements. It is necessary to tailor the Total Education and Training Plans to the achievement of company objectives.

By adopting this policy, the TQM education and training will become part of the company culture – a focal point for TQM which is always being updated and approved as new and better problem solving methods become available, or are developed internally. This will help the company achieve and maintain its competitive edge, through people.

STRUCTURE

The education requirement is to ensure everyone understands their role, and what is required of them. The measures established top-down in the organization should be included in the education and training material, to ensure full understanding of company objectives.

The training structure must be top-down, starting with the Top Team and cascading down the organization, as shown in

94 EDUCATION AND TRAINING

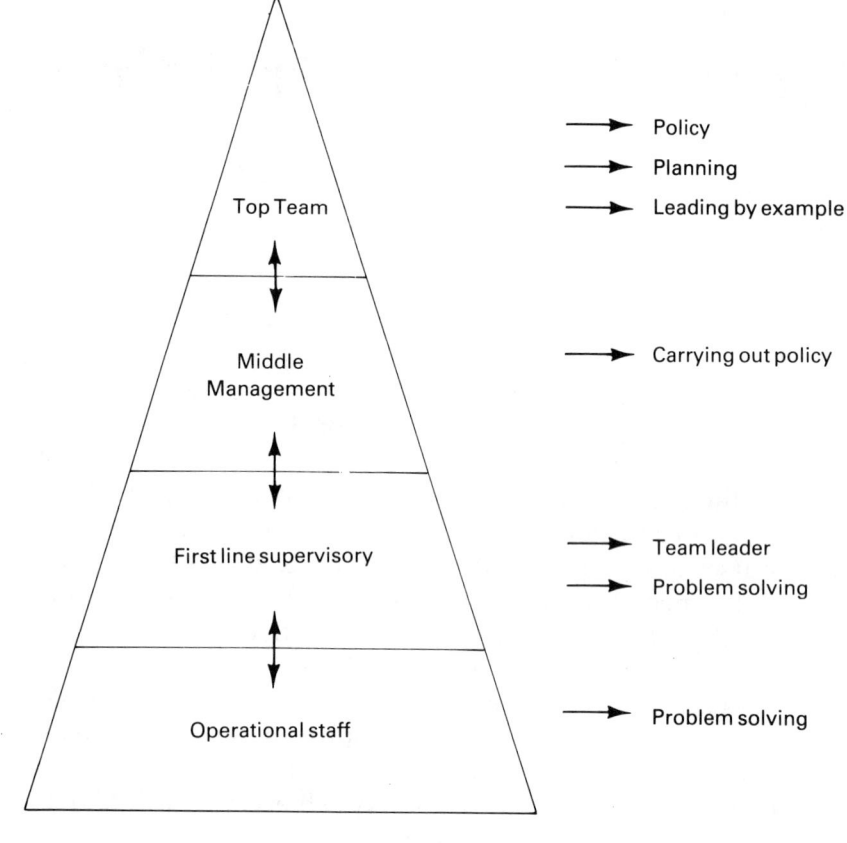

Figure 9.1 Top-down training structure.

Figure 9.1. The golden rule to successful implementation is to ensure managers train their own people. This is necessary to show management commitment, and to ensure managers actually understand the TQM principles and methods. After all, if you don't understand, you can't train. It also stops managers 'talking a good fight', and not actually fighting! In other words how can a manager continue with non-Quality methods when he's just trained and preached at people to adopt TQM principles.

PLANNING

The Top Team need to be trained before anyone else; in many cases this will require some external consultancy and training organization. Choosing the right people to do the job is of critical importance. The key selection criteria should be that the people understand the business the company is in and that the consultants chosen have a proven track record in TQM implementation in their own right. There is no substitute for experience when it comes to implementing a successful TQM process!

Clearly, the education and training planning is a key element of the overall TQM Quality improvement process. It is up to the Top Team member responsible for this element to ensure that his colleagues understand the 'top-down' policy, and take the opportunity to integrate the other clients of the Top Team plan with the education and training planning. For example:

1. **Management commitment**
   One of the best ways to demonstrate management commitment is for the managers to train their people.
2. **Measures**
   Using the education and training process to underline the importance of the measures used.
4. **Cost of Quality**
   Managers taking the opportunity to demonstrate to people during the training course, what has been achieved on Cost of Quality, what the corrective action teams are doing and so on.
4. **Quality improvement teams**
   Managers explaining the improvement team structure (Chapter 8), and taking the opportunity during the training course to encourage people to form or join continuous improvement teams. Again this shows management commitment.

Top Team
The need is to understand clearly the principles of TQM and plan the TQM implementation before launching the plan.

Team	Role	Course elements	Time
Top team	Policy planning	TQ principles Business strategy Performance measures	3 days
Middle management	Carrying out policy plans	TQ principles Business strategy Performance measures Team leadership Problem solving	5 days
First line	Problem solving team leader	TQ principles Team leadership Problem solving	5 days
Operations staff	Problem solving	TQ principles Problem solving	3 days

Figure 9.2 Total quality course structure.

Middle Management

To understand the principles of TQM, be aware of and contribute to the Top Team implementation plan. The Top Team need to take input from middle management and alter or modify the overall plan if necessary. This will help middle management commit to the whole process. This is a critical requirement as it is the middle management who will be mainly responsible for the training of the majority of people in the organization.

Therefore, the middle management training should include a heavy input from members of the Top Team. Courses need to be structured to meet three key requirements for middle management:

1. To understand TQM principles.
2. To renew the Top Team plan and agree implementation.
3. To develop a training course which will be suitable for the people who work for the middle management.

There is a lot of work to be done in any organization to meet these three requirements. The planning should be on iterative processes, whereby piloting of courses at all levels should be attempted and feedback obtained before fully committing the training plan.

One of the key contributors to success is the attitude of some of the middle management, when asked to do the training of their people; the response is normally:

'What me? I can't stand up in front of people and train them'.

This is a barrier that needs to be dismantled in two ways. The first is to explain quite clearly that this is a requirement in order to show management commitment, and that there can be no exceptions to this request. The second is to accept that there will be fears and concerns which need to be listened to and acted upon. For example, many people will need some help on presentation style and technique before 'going live'; this training will have to be provided for some of the middle management trainees.

It follows that the Education and Training Planning needs to be meticulous, detailed, and patient.

FACILITIES

It is no use starting the training off in a cramped Conference Room, or hastily organized training facility of some sort. This is Quality training, people are totally intolerant of anything which is not 'Quality'. To use the language – to meet their requirements. This means the provision of a training facility which looks and feels right, with decent furniture, full audio and visual equipment, and syndicate rooms for team working.

The facility should form a focus for Quality training and be established and maintained as such as a permanent requirement. It may be desirable to provide rooms in the same facility for the Quality improvement team to meet.

Administration support for the training is a key requirement – double booking of rooms is not allowable! This means the presence of full-time education and training facilitator and administration staff, ideally located in the Quality training facility.

EDUCATION AND TRAINING

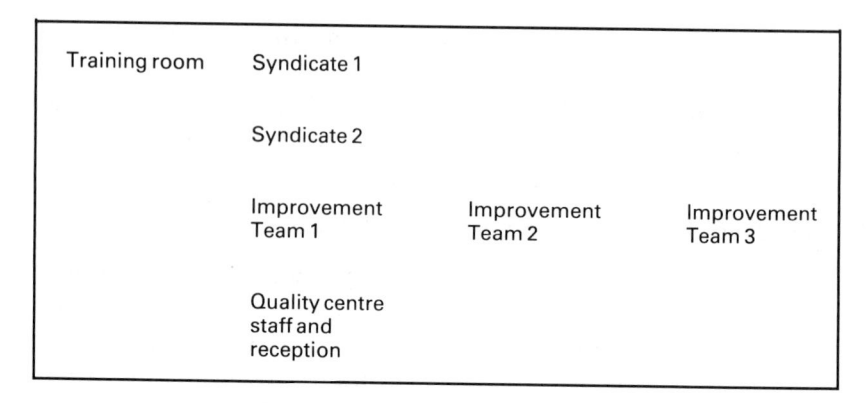

```
┌─────────────────────────────────────────────────────────────┐
│  Training room    Syndicate 1                               │
│                                                             │
│                   Syndicate 2                               │
│                                                             │
│                   Improvement    Improvement   Improvement  │
│                   Team 1         Team 2        Team 3       │
│                                                             │
│                   Quality centre                            │
│                   staff and                                 │
│                   reception                                 │
└─────────────────────────────────────────────────────────────┘
```

Figure 9.3 Typical quality training centre.

There is a need for a focal point for Quality, not only to ensure the training is carried out correctly, but also to provide a 'helpline' for individuals. For example, a trainee may want some 'quiet time' to produce a presentation, someone will want a measurement chart, and somebody else will want to see how a continuous improvement team works, before deciding to go ahead and form a team.

A typical layout for a Quality centre is shown in Figure 9.3.

PROBLEM SOLVING

The ability to solve problems is a key requirement of the continuous improvement process. The challenge is to ensure 100% of people are able to meet the requirements, throughout the organization.

There are three categories of problem solving:

1. Problem solving for everyone
2. Problem solving for teams
3. Problem solving for specialists

Taking each of these categories in turn:

Figure 9.4 'What do I do now?'

1. Problem solving for everyone

Training is required for 100% of people in the organization to learn the right approach to problem solving. This needs to be simple and effective so that it can easily be applied to everyday problems. It is not sensible to bombard people with '75 tools and techniques' of ranging complexity, which is an approach sometimes adopted by companies attempting to establish a problem solving capability in their people. The problem with this approach is that so much time is spent in learning the individual techniques that no time is left for understanding how to apply them!

The majority of problems can be solved with the technique described in this Chapter – simple, easy-to-use, and successful. Before describing the appropriate technique, however, there is an absolute requirement to understand the 'problem solving cycle'. The approach to problem solving which is required from 100% of people. It is essential that this problem solving cycle is fully understood before training people in tools and techniques, otherwise nobody will know when to use which technique. The problem with many tools and techniques courses is that, because the problem solving cycle is not fully explained or understood, people have great difficulty in understanding their application.

The problem solving cycle in Figure 9.5, and has four steps:

STEP 1 The first step is to clearly define the problem – to use the Japanese terminology 'What is the fact'. The temptation is to jump to conclusions without ever really studying the problem in the first place.

STEP 2 The second step is to analyse the information and establish the root cause problem.

STEP 3 The third step is to solve the problem by applying a corrective action, which meets the immediate requirement.

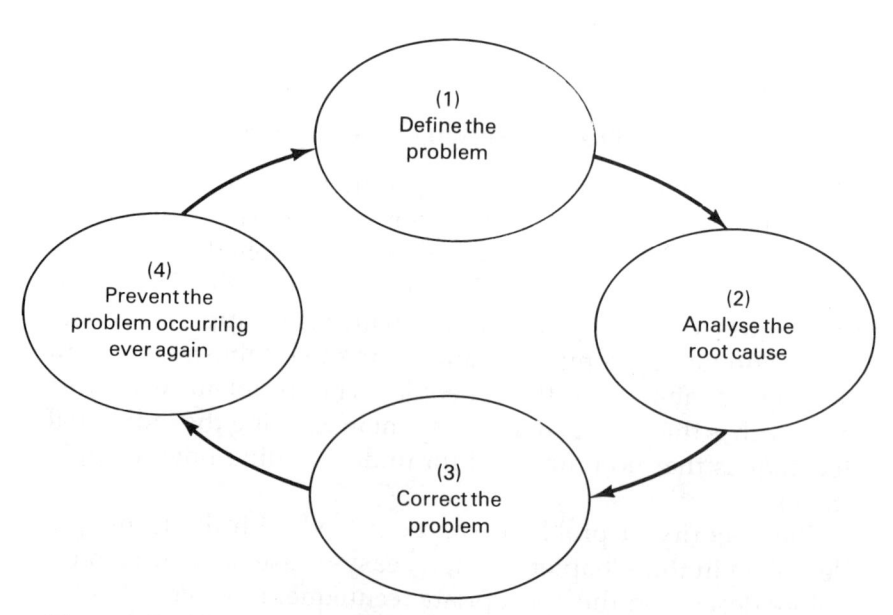

Figure 9.5 Four-step problem solving cycle.

STEP 4 The fourth step is to take the actions to ensure the problem can never occur again. This is very often different to Step 3 as it may mean a change to a process method, or system. It may be the promise of new or additional training, and better communication between people. This is the key prevention step; this problem should never be allowed to happen again.

When 100% of people think in this way there is an attitude of continuous improvement through problem solving. However, it is extremely frustrating for people to try to adopt this way of thinking and attacking problems if they are not given the tools and techniques to actually define the problem, or analyse the root cause. Part Three explains clearly the basic tools and techniques which can be used in the problem solving cycle.

2. Problem solving for teams

The problem solving cycle is applicable to teams of course, but the dynamics of problem solving are important to understand and continue. It is well known that the pooling of ideas and energy of like-minded people is a powerful method for resolving issues, and is more effective than a single shot by one person. However, it is important for the 'team' to be trained to act like a team! This is in addition to the tools and techniques training that all people will receive, and it should not be underestimated in importance. There is no value in a corrective action team, or continuous improvement team arguing about what is the most likely root cause, or 'whingeing' on about how poor Marketing are! Things cannot be done if some members of the team turn up late for the meetings, or don't turn up at all, if the meeting overruns or never starts on time. In short, there can be problems when you bring groups of individuals together.

What is needed is simple, basic training in team problem solving principles and techniques.

Principles of team problem solving

The first requirement is to observe good meetings discipline. This is applicable to all teams in the company, and especially the

Figure 9.6 Working together at board level.

Top Team, whose job it is to lead by example (see Figure 9.6). Sometimes it is not easy to remember, let alone with all the things that are necessary to be a successful team member!

The second requirement is to appoint a team leader for the CITs and CATs. It is the team leader's job to ensure everyone adheres to the meeting discipline, books the room, ensures everyone knows and keeps to time, keeps a record of actions and notes etc. It is also the team leader's job to facilitate the meeting. The facilitation job is to ensure the smooth running of the meeting, making sure everyone has their say, using a flip chart to record ideas. This is a leadership role and should be recognized as such. Training needs to be given to team leaders to enable them to facilitate team problem solving in the most efficient and practical way.

In the case of CITs and CATs the team leader will also provide the means of communication for the team upwards, across, or down the organization. The team leader in a corrective action team is often an imposed duty falling to the person recognized as the 'owner' of the problem. In a voluntary continuous improvement team, however, the leader is elected by the members, and then assumes the responsibilities of leader. This is often a fertile breeding ground for the emergence of potential supervisors or managers.

3. Problem solving for specialists

Up to 90% of all problems can be solved with simple, easy-to-use problem solving methods which everyone should learn and apply. However, there are always times when it will be difficult to define the problem clearly, or get to the root cause, or root causes. This is where specialist help is needed, and there is a requirement to train people who can offer this expertise when required.

From a management viewpoint in implementing Total Quality it is important to differentiate problem solving techniques, which everyone can learn and apply easily, from the specialist methods. There is no reason why a Top Team member should not become a specialist in one or more of the techniques. Indeed the ability to use the Relationship Diagram, for example, would be of immense use to the Top Team.

It is not possible or even advisable for me to state catagorically which techniques should be used by whom, or even at which stage of the problem solving cycle. The reality is that once capability and experience is established in the organization, it will become clear when to use the relevant techniques. Indeed as people get used to the use of the problem solving cycle, they will begin to look for new and improved tools and techniques, or those tools that specifically meet their requirement. A mature Quality organization will be aware of tools and techniques worldwide, will know when and how to apply them, and will also develop some tools and techniques of their own. This state of achievement is called:

'World class problem solving'

PROBLEM SOLVING SYSTEM

Even though everyone may be trained in problem solving techniques and understands the problem solving cycle it is a considerable help to have a system. This system is a simple, but formal method for the logging of a problem that the individual cannot solve on their own. The system must be available to everyone in the organization, who might otherwise be ignored.

The requirements of a problem solving system are:

Simplicity — the procedure should be easy to understand and follow.

Formality — there must be a written log of the problem.

Accountability — the problem needs to be 'given' to a person or team who agrees to solve the problem within an agreed timescale and to agreed results.

Co-ordination — problems and their solutions should be logged and made available to anyone in the organization. This ensures that if the same problem occurs again, there is a known solution which can be applied.

This requirement of known solutions can be tremendously effective in ensuring quick solutions of problems, and of course as information which allows prevention systems to be applied across the whole organization.

A typical problem solving form is shown in Figure 9.7. It is important to note that the individual must first talk to his or her immediate manager, and agree that the problem cannot be solved between them. This stops the system being abused by people who see it as a way of 'posting problems upwards!' Having agreed that the problem cannot be resolved at that level, a plan is drawn up identifying the person or persons who can solve the problem. This could mean the formation of a Corrective Action Team, or even a Continuous Improvement Team for example, or sometimes just a single person.

Agreement is needed between the originator and the problem solving group, or individual, who will need the originator's help in agreeing completion times and critical success factors.

```
┌─────────────────────────────────────────────────────────┐
│ ORIGINATOR:     ..........      EXTN:  ..........       │
│ REF NO:         ..........      DATE:  ..........       │
│ DIVISION/DEPT:  ..........                              │
│ SECTION:        ..........                              │
├─────────────────────────────────────────────────────────┤
│ WHAT IS THE PROBLEM?:                                   │
│                                                         │
│                                                         │
│                                                         │
│                                                         │
│ CLASSIFICATION: T/P/N                                   │
├─────────────────────────────────────────────────────────┤
│ ACTIONEE .............................................. │
│ AGREED FORECAST COMPLETION DATE ..............          │
│ ACTION TAKEN:                                           │
│                                                         │
│                                                         │
│                                                         │
│                                                         │
│                                                         │
│                                                         │
│                                                         │
│ SIGNED OFF BY ORIGINATOR ..........  DATE ........      │
└─────────────────────────────────────────────────────────┘
```

Figure 9.7 Problem solving log.

Prevention of problems

Once a formula for logging problems and their solutions is in place, there is a tremendous amount of information available to the organization on better ways of doing things. For example, a method for ensuring the telephone is always answered within three rings in a sales office might be developed in one location as a result of a problem logged. The problem might be a lost order! Once this improved system has been implemented in that office, there must be a mechanism and clearly the same system is applied to all the sales offices across the organization. This can be achieved if the problem and solution is logged and available to the organization at all levels. It is up to the problem solving Top Team member to devise a system to enable this to happen across the organization.

CHAPTER TEN

Involvement and commitment

'Acceptance and understanding is a pre-requisite to obtaining the whole-hearted commitment of people.'

TIMING

The timing of communication to the organization regarding TQM progress is critical. It is tempting but wrong to hold a major launch explaining what is going to happen on TQM, before the Top Team is actually educated and into the planning. There are two reasons for holding off until a little later.

The first reason is that an expectation of change and improvement will be given to the people in the organization without the capability to meet this expectation. This will lead to disappointment and cynicism and reflect badly on the integrity and capability of the Top Team.

The second reason is that there will be no 'common language' amongst the Top Team members, which will lead to the conclusion that 'they are not working together and just don't know what they are talking about'.

As explained in Chapter 9 – Education and Training, the top-down nature of the education and training process allows an excellent opportunity to fully explain what the TQM process is about, what it is expected to achieve for the organization, and the individual's role in the Continuous Improvement Process. It follows, therefore, that the Top Team should work closely within the team education and training to ensure successful implementation. In this respect it is important for the Top Team to be fully educated in TQM, and be into the planning of its implementation, before considering a TQM launch. This will ensure all the Top Team members are seen to understand what they are talking about. It will also 'feel real' to the people in the organization when the Top Team talk in detail about the planning, the structure, the approach to training, and so on. There will be facts, and plans including timescales etc., and a clear indication of how everyone will be involved in the TQM continuous improvement process.

COMMUNICATION METHODS

As the TQM planning starts, and the Cost of Quality corrective action teams begin to make an impact, there will be a requirement to formally communicate the TQM plans.

There are two actions that lead to a successful launch of these plans to the organization.

The first is to prepare a TQM Presentation which should be given by the appropriate Top Team member to their people. This presentation needs to be prepared by the Top Team and fully agreed and understood by all Top Team members. It is important that the same messages are given by all the Top Team to ensure accuracy, credibility and commitment.

The second action is to prepare a quality newsletter which is the written record of the launch presentation. It is a good idea to maintain production of the quality newsletter, as a means of written communication on the TQM plan progress.

TQM launch presentation

The planning of the presentation should be meticulous in terms of time, location and Top Team participation. It is essential for one or more of the Top Team members to actually give the presentation, but for all of the Top Team to be able to understand and answer the questions which will follow. This launch should only take place with the total Top Team agreement.

Management style

All the TQM launches and quality newsletters will be useless, of course, if the management style is not open, and leadership is not given to the people. It follows that, as I have stated before, all managers must be trained in the TQM principles and problem solving methods, so that they can actually help their people continuously improve. Again, even if the managers are experts on problem solving this is not likely to be of much use if his or her management style is not conducive to two-way communication. The shortest way I can describe the requirement is to ask all managers to follow the GOYA principle.

GOYA principle

GET OFF YOUR A***!!!!!!!

'It's amazing what you learn by talking to people!'
'It's also frightening and humbling to realize how much you don't know.'

RECOGNITION AND REWARD

As the TQM Quality improvement process is implemented 'Quality Champions' will emerge. These are people who are outstanding in their attitudes, dedication, and commitment to Quality. They fight the cynics, even when they may be at management level! It is important to recognize who these people are, and to ensure some means of reward to them. This will help to give these 'Quality Champions' more confidence and provide a culture of recognition for the right people.

Identifying who these people are is not as easy as it might seem. Traditionally, the people who have been rewarded are the best 'fire-fighters', even though in some cases they are the same people who 'started the fires' in the first place! The requirement is to look closely at the Quality Policy and set of values which comprise the Quality culture, and calibrate people's performance and attitude against these criteria. For example, how much time is spent in successfully preventing problems occurring? Compare this with the amount of time spent in correcting problems, i.e. 'fire-fighting'. What is the rate of uptake of continuous improvement teams in a department or section? How many problems are being noted and solved in a department or section?

It is all about personal commitment; some individuals will become determined to succeed whilst others will adopt a 'wait and see' attitude. Those individuals who are determinedly committed to the successful implementation of the Quality improvement process are worth their weight in gold! They will appear at every level of the organization and need to be encouraged and supported by management. It is management's role to ensure the right people are recognized, the people who are walking demonstrations of the Quality Policy.

It is particularly important to provide encouragement and support in the early stages of TQM implementation, in order to make it absolutely clear that management are serious about TQM. Recognizing and rewarding the 'Quality Champions' sends the right signals down the organization, and will help to ensure the rest of the people understand the new set of values which the organization has adopted through TQM. The main reason for recognizing and rewarding people is to ensure the correct values are understood in the organization.

Methods of reward for individuals

'Quality Champions' can be rewarded in a number of ways. Basically the question is whether to reward financially or otherwise! This depends on the organization and the decision must be made by the Top Team only after considerable time and discussions have taken place. The dangers of financial reward are that it could be dangerously divisive, yet correcting it would have the effect of ensuring people 'take seriously' the management initiative on TQM. There is no simple answer to this question, it depends on the type of business, organization, whether suggestion schemes exist or not, and so on. If financial incentives are given it is sensible to keep them to reasonable levels, major financial rewards will certainly cause divisions and inhibit teamwork. Perhaps non-financial incentives could also lead to discussion – for example it is not a good idea to reward a 'Quality Champion' with a Rolls-Royce! How do you follow that? Do lesser 'Quality Champions' get a smaller car, or even a bicycle!

I don't believe it is necessary to adopt a policy of giving high-value rewards in order to ensure that 'Quality Champions' are recognized. The fact that they are recognized at all is the key factor; the tangible reward can be something relatively low value but useful. For example, calculators, pens, watches, bags, etc. are very well received and appreciated by people who have been recognized as 'Quality Champions'. These types of rewards, which are visible, useful, and practical, are not likely to cause divisions, but will be appreciated by the recipients. It is a fundamental aspect of the individual's commitment to the Quality improvement process, that the person will want to do the job right even without a reward. This is the culture that the organization is fighting to establish – the key requirement if individual recognition and reward is that the right people are recognized – not the value of the reward.

Day to day management role

There can be a temptation at Top Team level to consider that once a recognition and reward policy and system has been established then the work is complete. It is easy to forget that the primary purpose of the recognition and reward system is to ensure that the individuals who demonstrate commitment to the Quality Policy are recognized, and given encouragement and support. This helps underpin the TQM implementation process.

Ensuring the right people are recognized is probably the toughest task facing the Top Team. Each manager must ensure that he or she knows the people in his department/section. This can only be achieved by adopting the GOYA Principle described in the previous Chapter! In other words taking time out every day to walk the office, or the shop floor, asking questions, judging attitudes and commitment. It will not be difficult to make a judgement on who the quality champions are as well! The method for nominating quality champions needs to be discussed and agreed by the Top Team, but only when each Manager has formed a value judgement on the people and attitudes prevailing in his department, section, or organization. It is essential to have this 'gut feel' before deciding on the method of nomination. For example, is it going to be a peer group nomination, or maybe nominations by each manager? How do you know the selecting manager is using the correct criteria? Is there a 'blue-eyed boy syndrome'? All of these factors and many more need to be discussed before agreeing to the method of nomination. Whatever method is chosen, the key requirement is that it is fair, and <u>seen</u> <u>to</u> <u>be</u> <u>fair</u>.

Recognition and reward for teams

It is possible to extend the individual recognition and reward systems to successful teams. For example, Continuous Improvement Teams or Corrective Action Teams who have successfully completed a project may qualify for a reward. This could be on the successful completion of every project – say two per year, or on the first successful project the team completes. Rewards could be the same tokens given to individuals, where each member of the team receives a pen, or watch, for example. Alternatively there may be a case for rewarding the team by giving the members and their partners theatre tickets, or dinner, for example. This idea helps to mature the team spirit of the members.

There may be the opportunity for all the Continuous Improvement Teams, or Corrective Action Teams to enter their project for an annual award given by the organization for the 'Top Quality Team'. This event would take the format of the teams presenting their work to a 'panel of judges' who would decide the top team based on an agreed set of requirements. The reward for this team could be to represent the organization at National or even International Conferences. It could be an overseas study and exchange tour of organizations in other countries, Europe, Japan, USA, etc. The reward criteria here is status, and recognition that the Top Quality Team has an ambassadorial role on behalf of all the people in the organization. This type of approach is a powerful motivation to the 'Quality Champions'.

Building on this recognition and reward method for teams, it is beneficial to organize exchange visits with other TQM organizations. In these visits team members get the opportunity to talk to other 'Quality Champions' from different organizations. The process is interesting, educational and lifts the spirits of team members, who may be solving difficult issues and problems. Opportunities should be taken to send as many quality teams as possible to external events, such as quality conferences and courses. It is essential in these cases to ask each team to write a short report on their views of the conference, with suggestions for actions that could be taken by the organization to improve the implementation of TQM. This type of approach keeps the whole process going – it keeps people's interest and is a vehicle for continuous improvement.

Recognition and reward as part of education and training

Every single person in the organization will be trained in the TQM Quality Improvement Process. As people complete the course, the signing of the Quality Policy and the presentation of the Policy as a reward for completing the course is a powerful method of recognition and reward. It may be advantageous to include the Quality Policy with a 'Certificate of Achievement' on completion of the course.

A typical certificate would look like that one shown in Fig. 10.1. This type of reward certificate approach incorporated with the Quality Policy is a powerful reinforcement of the Quality message, particularly if the certificate is framed. This allows the framed certificate to be put in the individual's work area, either on the desk or the wall. It can be seen that in this way the TQM Quality Improvement Process is becoming part of the culture – literally in or on the walls of the organization! Having the signed

---

RECOGNITION CERTIFICATE

THIS IS TO CERTIFY THAT ....
HAS ATTENDED A TRAINING COURSE IN
TOTAL QUALITY CONTINUOUS
IMPROVEMENT.

SIGNED ....

I AM TOTALLY COMMITTED TO CONTINUOUS
IMPROVEMENT.

SIGNED ....

Figure 10.1 Recognition/Reward certificate.

Quality Policy/certificate of achievement is a constant reminder of the individual's commitment to Quality, and a visible commitment throughout the organization.

Profit sharing

The TQM Quality Improvement Process implemented successfully will generate increased profit for the organization. Who should share in these profits? Surely there should be a method for ensuring everyone in the organization shares in the financial successes in an equitable manner. This is probably one of the hardest issues to tackle for a successful company. There are many methods, including a bonus based on salary, across the board bonus applied equally to everyone in the organization, or share ownership.

Of all the methods, probably the one which fits the ethics and long-term requirements, of the TQM Quality Improvement Process is the Share Ownership Scheme.

The idea of everyone in the organization owning shares and therefore working for the organization as a shareholder is not new. However, the opportunity to either give or offer shares at reduced rates, is worthy of serious consideration as a means of rewarding success.

CHAPTER ELEVEN

Supplier strategy

There are few businesses where there is no reliance on an external supplier, or suppliers. This applies to industrial companies who purchase material, add value to it and sell to their customers. It also applies to the service industries who rely on sub-contract staff, or third party suppliers for food, laundry, cleaning, catering, etc.

Take the example of a hotel which is offering conference facilities, and is relying on an audio-visual company to supply the projector. It is no use blaming that company if the equipment arrives late, or it is not the equipment asked for by the customer. The customer's contact is with the hotel, not the audio-visual company. It is this realization that there is a critical dependency on suppliers which forces the need for application of TQM into the supplier base.

DEFINITION OF SUPPLIER

In this context it is any external supplier – that is to say a person, or organization supplying a service or product to the company. This includes companies who supply material, components, products etc., to which the company adds value before selling on to the customer. It is almost impossible to find a company or business that does not depend on this type of supplier. It also includes sub-contractors and suppliers who provide a service to the company, which is then sold on to the customer.

Then, of course, there is the area of facilities management – the provision of support services to the company. This includes cleaning, catering, mailing distribution and transport, and so on. Facilities management has become very big business where many companies have been formed to provide a complete portfolio of services. It is becoming increasingly critical for companies to develop and apply a clear TQM supplier strategy.

TQM SUPPLIER STRATEGY

The strategy is simple for the suppliers – 'To adopt exactly the same TQM policy, attitudes, and actions required of the company'. This means that every supplier to the company must adopt the same TQM principles and Quality culture. If this isn't the case, the company can never achieve the business objectives targeted through continuous improvement. It follows that every supplier must be assessed, and their ability to meet the TQM policies and requirements clearly qualified.

What is required is a joint company/supplier commitment to TQM. This joint approach can only work when the company and supplier personnel work together to meet agreed requirements. This approach requires time and effort on both sides. Existing supplier relationships must be examined, for example, is it the company purchasing policy to keep a large number of suppliers for a particular product or service, and 'play one off against the other'. This type of approach may succeed in knocking down the incoming costs, but who is to say that a long-term Purchasing Agreement with, say two suppliers, would not achieve the same cost reductions. It is a strong negotiating point to offer maybe yearly or even longer contracts to suppliers and it is normal to achieve good cost reductions with this type of approach. However, the other major benefit, of course, is the ability to develop a joint TQM understanding with suppliers, which results in a long-term business partnership. It isn't possible to develop a long-term business partnership with suppliers if they are being 'played off against each other', and if there is therefore little prospect of long-term contracts. Clearly the TQM approach means that the purchasing policy in the company must be reviewed, and in many cases changed from a multi-supplier base for the same product/service to a single or double supplier only.

In fact it is impossible to achieve world class performance without developing the same type of continuous improvement policy with suppliers as in the organization. The same principles apply which are outlined in this book, but practically of course, and it is necessary to reduce the supplier base to manageable levels.

This is first achieved through the supplier assessment procedure; the reduction of the supplier base is a key activity in TQM implementation and must be very carefully executed. It will take time and effort, involving the careful qualification of every supplier to the company. The suppliers will need to be categorized after assessment into the following levels:

Supplier status

Approved	:	Supplier meets all requirements
Conditionally approved	:	Supplier agrees to correct deficiencies found
Failed	:	Unacceptable supplier

This simple categorization will have the effect of reducing the supplier base into manageable types. The approved supplier will be to the desired Total Quality standard requiring continuous improvement actions. The conditionally approved will require education and training, whilst the failed should be taken off the supplier base.

Supplier assessment process

This process is a well-defined set of requirements which need to be thoroughly understood within the company, before specify-

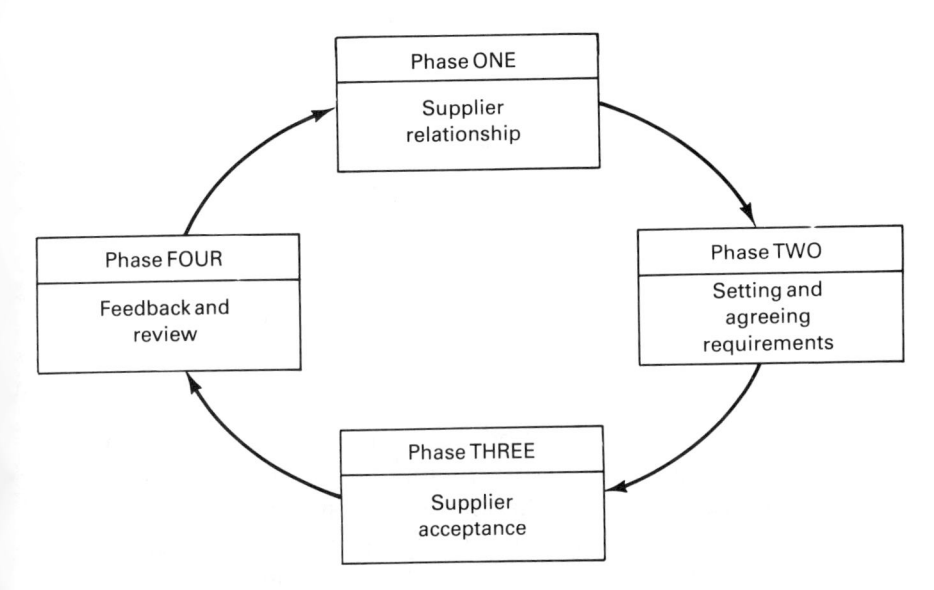

Figure 11.1 Supplier assessment cycle.

ing them to the suppliers. It can best be described as a four-phase cycle as shown in Figure 11.1.

Justifying TQM supplier strategy

The development and implementation of the TQM supplier strategy takes time and effort. It is an investment in the prevention of error and a true Cost of Conformance. It should not be seen as an added cost, but as a means of reducing the Cost of Non-conformance. The Cost of Quality work within the company will identify clearly the importance of the TQM supplier strategy.

CHAPTER TWELVE

Time to market

There is a major difference between the Japanese approach to design, and traditional Western methods – TQM principles, have been applied to the Japanese process, whereas typically there has been a total lack of TQM application in the West. The failure to apply TQM principles results in the serial approach to design, which forces the design process through the functional departments in the organization. For example, in basic terms:

Marketing specification
↓
Design and development
↓
Manufacture
↓
Sales

In this type of approach it is left to each department to complete their individual part of the process, largely in solution, before handing on to the next department. Typically there is little communication between the departments, except where handing over from department to another. At this stage there is usually plenty of communication but unfortunately it can often follow the lines of the following:

'Between Design and Manufacture'.

Manufacturing: 'How do you expect me to put this product through my production line with this new design. I haven't got the right equipment.'

Design: 'Well, I didn't know that, nobody told me!'

The blame for this all too common situation lies firmly and squarely on both Design and Manufacturing. It is no use Design complaining that Manufacturing people are 'greasy oily characters who screw up my design'. Equally it is no use Manufacturing claiming that Design people are 'smart-a.. characters who wouldn't know one end of the production line from the other'. It is ludicrous to think that Marketing, Design, Manufacture, or Sales could be completed in the serial manner just described, but that's exactly what happens typically in the West.

Of course it is not as simple as this – in most cases there is a complete lack of understanding of what actually goes on in a company at each interface level, whereby management monitors the success of new product introduction, and the ability to complete each phase within the targeted time. In other words, the Product Introduction Meeting concentrates on the time targets, much more than the produce and customer requirement. This leads to an attitude in each department to 'get rid' of their part of the product introduction process as soon as possible. Marketing will want to 'get rid' to design as soon as they can. Design will want to hand over to Manufacturing, again as soon as possible – particularly if the design is not technically challenging any more – and has become boring! Manufacturing, of course, will want to output the product, no matter how, to meet the pressure from sales.

Unfortunately, when the customer, who has largely been forgotten throughout this process, gets the product it doesn't actually do what he expected it to do! The result of this is obvious; the customer is not satisfied, and goes elsewhere the next time.

The scenario I have just described has been enacted hundreds, if not thousands of times throughout the Western world during the last 30 years or so. The main beneficiaries of this situation have been, of course, the Japanese who have managed to get their products to the market and meeting or exceeding the customer's requirements. In the case of television sets in the 1970s, they set a whole new standard for reliability which far exceeded the customer's expectations. No wonder they have been successful.

THE SIMPLE ANSWERS

There is a simple answer to the problem of getting products to the market and meeting the requirement of customers, and also, of course, meeting gross margin targets necessary to be successful as a company. The answer is to totally change the management view of the product introduction methods away from departmental responsibilities to total responsibilities of the people involved throughout the whole process.

The business of getting products to the marketplace must be viewed as a 'total process', completely independent of the functional departments existing in the company. It is disastrous to 'shoe-horn' new product process requirements into the existing departmental structure of the organization. It is also disastrous for management to consider that there could possibly be anything as simple as the design process completed by the Design department, or the manufacturing process completed by the Manufacturing department. Getting products to market is not a simple, serial process, whose individual and very specific knowledge and experience exist solely within departmental barriers. How can the people in Manufacturing not have an input at the Design and Development stage? How can the Sales teams have no contribution to make at the marketing specification stage? After all they do talk to the customers!

This compartmentalized thinking by management totally fails to realize that everyone involved at each stage of the process must be involved from the beginning right through to the end. This is the simple answer to the success of competing with the Japanese. It is not a new idea, so why hasn't it happened in the West? The answer to this question is very much what the book is all about – only through the application of TQM can Western companies hope to compete with the Far Eastern machines.

TQM applied to the product market process

It is essential to use the problem solving cycle at top level to provide a common understanding within the Top Team of the product introduction process. The problem solving cycle is the core process that is used throughout the product introduction procedure. This strategy is based on the understanding that it is not possible to ever achieve a situation where there are no problems to address throughout the product introduction process. A sentiment I am sure anyone reading this book who has been directly involved in product introduction will whole-heartedly agree with! It follows, therefore, that there must be a common approach to the elimination of problems by everyone involved in the product introduction process.

Through TQM everyone will understand and be able to apply the problem solving cycle, which provides a common language and common understanding totally independent of department or functions. At Top Team level it is necessary to use the cycle to determine how the product introduction procedure should be defined, maintained and controlled. This could affect the way the company is organized, whether to 'make or buy', to set up a new factory, to organize new distribution capabilities, to acquire new business to support the product in a new market or new country, and so on. Whatever decisions are made during the defining of requirements stage, there will be the need to apply the problem solving cycle for as long as the product is being marketed and sold.

At each stage in the development of product introduction process using the problem solving cycle the following questions should be asked:

1. What is the requirement/problem?
2. Who must be involved in defining the requirements or solving the problems?

3. Who is responsible for ensuring requirements are met or executed?

If this procedure is followed it is possible to define the product introduction requirement at each stage, who is involved in defining and agreeing them, and who is responsible for meeting them.

This approach will avoid the pitfall of designing a product introduction procedure around functional barriers. It will ensure everyone understands their role in the process, and provide the foundation for a 'team approach'. The problem solving cycle must be applied to each stage in product introduction.

Stage 1: Define market requirement

This is typically the first phase in the product introduction process. It is not possible to provide a clear market requirement at this stage in isolation within the Marketing department. Inputs must be sought from representatives at each stage of the product introduction process that is to say, from Design, Manufacturing,

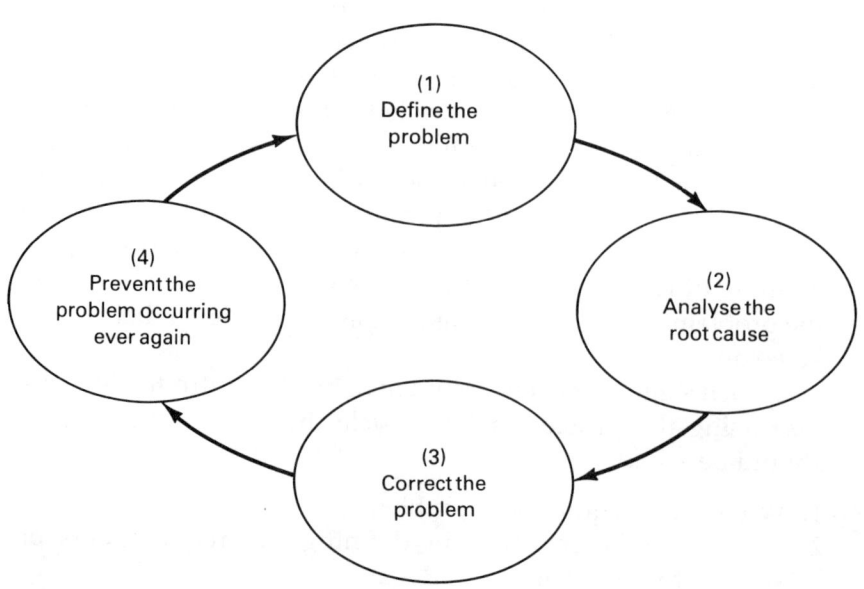

Figure 12.1 Problem solving cycle.

Sales, Finance, etc. It is up to the Top Team to define clearly the need for Marketing to follow this procedure.

This is an iterative process where the broad requirements specified by Marketing will be subjected to the cycle of:

Analyse   : Analysing requirement
Correction : Correcting errors
Prevention: Preventing problems reaching the later stages of design, manufacturing, sales, customer service, etc.

When the Team has obtained an agreed market specification, it is possible to decide whether to proceed to the next stage. This should be agreed at a formal Phase Review where representatives for each area of the company propose the recommended course of action to the Top Team. There is no reason why it should be only the Marketing department who make this recommendation – the TQM principles demand that it is a team approach, and therefore 'team commitment'.

The involvement of design, manufacturing and sales production people at this stage will obtain their commitment to the success of the product throughout the product introduction process. It will teach them that it is an iterative process, and impossible to define clearly a market requirement that will never change. Market requirements change constantly; it is the company that understands this and is organized and committed to the management of change that will be successful.

Stage 2: Product definition requirement

The requirement is to complete detailed planning, including technical specification project plans, etc. Again the problem solving cycle must be used by the team to ensure that the product definition is understood and agreed to by all people concerned.

Stage 3: Design and development

This stage is to demonstrate the ability to meet the requirements specified in the previous two stages. The problem solving cycle will be used to analyse problems, correct them, and then ensure that they don't happen again. For example, correcting problems found in a power supply design, should be carried out on the product which is the third stage in the problem solving cycle. However, it is necessary to go one stage further to stage 4, and prevent the problem occurring again by, for example, committing the change to engineering standards. Therefore, this knowledge is captured for ever, and will become the company standard to be used in future.

There is a heavy involvement with suppliers at this stage of the product introduction process, and they must be seen as integral members of the 'product introduction team'. Again the suppliers will be committed to the problem solving cycle, to ensure the ability to continuously improve the product. The team approach to Design and Development, and the 100% application of the problem solving cycle will ensure maximum efficiency in progressing through this critical stage; and to the successful progression to stage 4.

Stage 4: Field trial and full-scale manufacture
This is the most critical of stages in one respect. That is because there is nobody between the product and the customer! Again the problem solving cycle will be used before the product is considered to be capable of meeting customers requirements in the marketplace.

Stage 5: Mature product requirement
This is the process of reviewing continuously the performance of the product in the marketplace. It will give the opportunity to consider whether to sell into different countries, different markets, modify the product to provide a further revenue stream, etc.

It is beneficial to use the problem solving cycle to define the requirement of the product in meeting company business targets. Then, to analyse the problems and opportunities, with the object of reducing cost, increasing marketplace, etc. Then, to correct the problems, or take advantage of the opportunities, the final stage of prevention is to use all the knowledge and information gained to prevent problems occurring again. This is the process of continuous improvement applied to the product introduction process in the company. It must be reviewed, and improved upon in the company at regular intervals and the problem solving cycle must be applied throughout the total process, ensuring the involvement of the people in the organization at every stage. The old traditional and failed ideas must be thrown out, to be replaced by the TQM approach to produce introduction. The ideas in this chapter are specifically aimed at getting this message across, and are absolutely essential to achieve success in the world marketplace. It will provide the capability to continuously improve through commitment, involvement and determination of all the people in the organization.

CHAPTER THIRTEEN

Organizational design

CULTURE

After many years' experience of implementing Total Quality into organizations large and small, and across different businesses, one key issue has become increasingly obvious and constant. The organizational culture is the main reason why Total Quality Management is required for companies to meet the competitive challenge by focussing on customers' requirements. The previous chapters in this book give a straightforward approach for the heads of companies to adopt which will provide a customer focus in their organization.

It is worth asking the question 'Why is this book of any value to the Chief Executive Officer of any company?' – or if you prefer 'What is the value of Total Quality to any company and why is it required?' The answer to these questions lies in the nature of the organizational design companies adopt. It is an organizational design which is hierarchical and top-down typically in information flows with many functional groups and 'managers' at many levels.

This organizational design is adopted because it is necessary to create management control and accountability top-down throughout the company. Without it nobody can see who they work for, there would be no effective review of performance, and no clear lines of communication. It is an organizational style adopted where many companies have demonstrated excellent management control at all levels of the hierarchy. Training at all levels has been dissected, leadership skills enhanced and management information systems implemented to give top management the information needed to control the company. So how could so many companies with an excellent management organization and control of information have such a difficult time competing in world markets? What is wrong with this traditional hierarchical approach? The answer, strangely enough, is nothing at all!

It is essential for all companies to adopt a structure which will give good management control and clear lines of communication and accountability. The problem does not lie in the fundamental organizational structure that companies adopt but in the mistaken belief that somehow this 'internally' focussed organization will automatically be satisfactory for meeting 'external' requirements.

These external requirements get in the way of the internally focussed organization because information flow and material flow go horizontally across the organization and not vertically as is the case with internal management information and control. Look at the focus companies have internally.

1. All CEOs can easily reel off their organization structure.
2. Most Directors' time is spent in internal organization of resources.
3. Most 'management' time is spent preparing information for senior management.
4. Most meetings are concerned with meeting internally focussed measures.
5. The most important measures in the organization are financial by a long way.

Approximately only 10% of time is spent on external focus.

1. How many CEOs have a mission statement?
2. How many Boards have clear 'business drivers'?
3. How many Boards understand the key performance measures required of their company to ensure customer satisfaction?
4. How much time do top management spend talking to their customers?

5. How much time do senior management spend doing competitive benchmarking – finding out about their competition and emulating best practice?
6. How much time is spent in defining, measuring and monitoring the performance measures which are critical to meeting customer requirements?
7. How much time is spent ensuring everyone in the organization has a customer focus and clear performance measures?

The list of questions is long and depressing for it is a fact that most companies do not spend any more than 10% of their management time focussing on customer requirements. It is little wonder that companies demonstrating this internal view of life sooner or later meet severe competition problems. Many companies in the manufacturing business have clearly found this out too late and some companies in the service sector are beginning to realize that there is a better way of spending management time. For those who do not realize these cold, hard facts of life, there is only one way to go – OUT OF BUSINESS.

Sooner or later another company will begin to meet customers' requirements better and will force the less externally focussed to go out of business.

ARE YOU AN INTERNALLY OR EXTERNALLY FOCUSSED COMPANY?

Internally focussed organizational cultures

- Unclear who the customers are.
- No performance measures reflecting customer requirements.
- No good personal relationship built up with the customer.
- No understanding of the customer's business.
- Complete lack of understanding of external customers within the workforce.
- Meetings cultures where senior management spend up to 90% of their time in meetings, mainly on internal measures, or on dissatisfied customers!

- Poorly run and ineffective meetings, where no actions are agreed, decisions are made on very little information in case the facts get in the way!
- Poor morale and commitment at all levels.
- Enormous amount of senior management time deciding on the 'structure' of the organization – with external customers' requirements <u>never</u> coming into the discussions.

Externally focussed organizational cultures

- Pro-active attempts to define customers' requirements through understanding of the customers' business.
- Good problem-solving skills particularly at the customer interface, involving education of the customers' staff where necessary.
- Exactly the same approach as above for suppliers, seeing them as 'part of the business'.
- Clear mission statement and business drivers.
- Clearly defined performance measures reflecting customers' requirements.
- Everyone in the organization understands the internal customer concept and has performance measures agreed reflecting the external customer needs.
- There is a positive approach to problem solving and open discussion on how to resolve problems.
- High morale due to the customer focus and positive attempts at solving problems at all levels throughout the organization.

MAKING THE TRANSFORMATION TO A TQM ORGANIZATION

Nothing will change unless the CEO realizes that there is a transformation needed. Very often, particularly when companies are demonstrating good financial results, there is a tendency to 'leave things alone'. This approach would work well if nothing else changed as well! Unfortunately there is nothing so certain

132   ORGANIZATIONAL DESIGN

as change. This means that companies must always be looking for ways of improving their products/service, constantly re-evaluating their markets and competitors and prepared for unforeseen worldwide events which can spark a recession. Providing the company is geared to external change factors, then it is possible for the organization to respond faster, and more

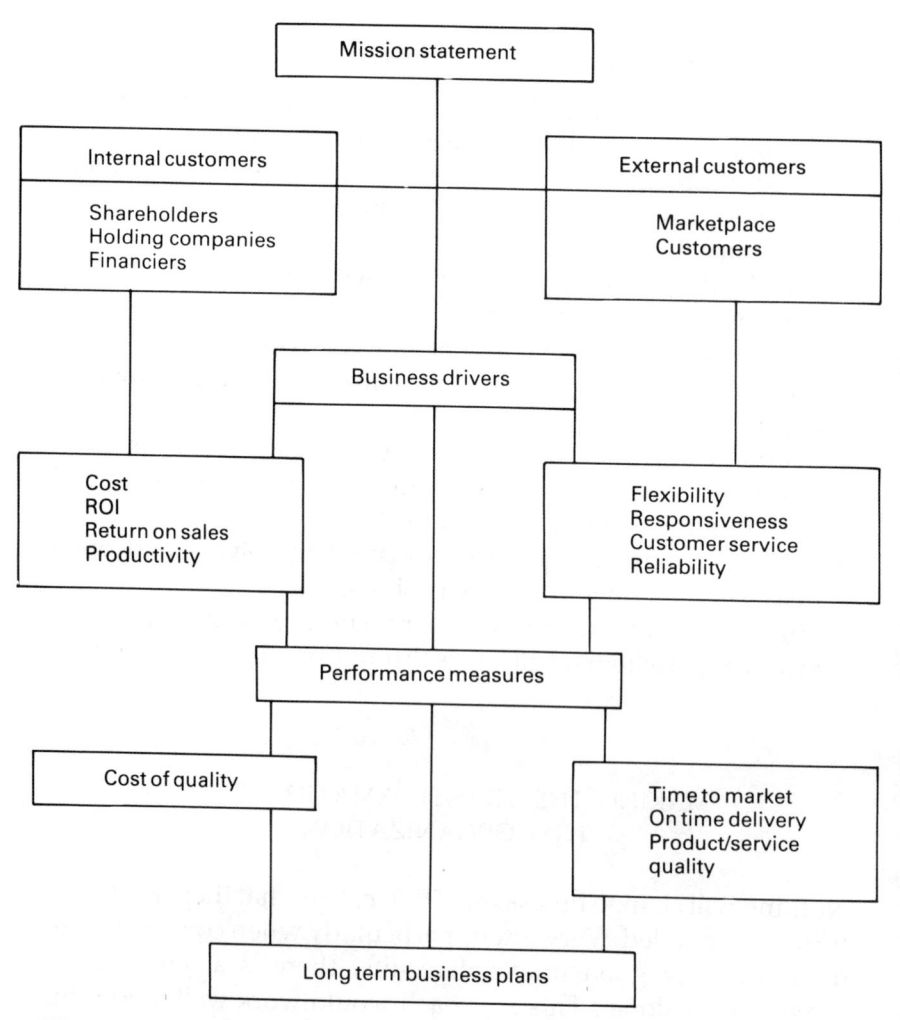

```
                    ┌─────────────────────┐
                    │  Mission statement  │
                    └──────────┬──────────┘
                               │
    ┌──────────────────┐       │       ┌──────────────────┐
    │ Internal customers│      │       │ External customers│
    ├──────────────────┤       │       ├──────────────────┤
    │ Shareholders     │       │       │ Marketplace      │
    │ Holding companies│       │       │ Customers        │
    │ Financiers       │       │       │                  │
    └────────┬─────────┘       │       └────────┬─────────┘
             │                 │                │
             │        ┌────────┴────────┐       │
             │        │ Business drivers│       │
             │        └────────┬────────┘       │
             │                 │                │
    ┌────────┴─────────┐       │       ┌────────┴─────────┐
    │ Cost             │       │       │ Flexibility      │
    │ ROI              │       │       │ Responsiveness   │
    │ Return on sales  │       │       │ Customer service │
    │ Productivity     │       │       │ Reliability      │
    └────────┬─────────┘       │       └────────┬─────────┘
             │                 │                │
             │       ┌─────────┴──────────┐     │
             │       │Performance measures│     │
             │       └─────────┬──────────┘     │
             │                 │                │
    ┌────────┴────────┐        │       ┌────────┴─────────┐
    │ Cost of quality │        │       │ Time to market   │
    └────────┬────────┘        │       │ On time delivery │
             │                 │       │ Product/service  │
             │                 │       │ quality          │
             │                 │       └────────┬─────────┘
             │                 │                │
             │       ┌─────────┴──────────┐     │
             └───────┤Long term business plans├─┘
                     └────────────────────┘
```

Figure 13.1 Spenley business process.

successfully than the competition. History has shown that those companies which are externally focussed always provide a more perceptive, flexible and competitive response to change than the internally focussed, rather complacent companies.

This understanding of the unpredictability of some external factors should be enough to convince all CEOs of the need for change, quite apart from the obvious sense of keeping close to the customers' requirements. When the CEO is convinced that an externally focussed company is sharper, faster and more competitive, then the transformation process from internal to external can begin. The Spenley Business Strategy Model in Figure 13.1 shows how the organization should act to link the elements of strategy.

THE ROLES OF THE QUALITY MANAGER AND THE TOTAL QUALITY MANAGER

One of the problems of using the words Total Quality management is the expectation from Quality professionals that this is in their area of responsibility. After all, it must be the Quality manager's job to put in Total Quality – who else is responsible? It is essential to understand that Total Quality has no more or less to do with the Quality manager than the sales manager, production manager, commercial manager, or any other manager!

It follows, therefore, that the existing Quality manager should basically get on with implementing Total Quality along with all his or her colleagues on the Top Team. In other words, the role of the Total Quality manager is _totally_ different to the role of the traditional Quality manager in the organization. The reasons for this should be clear after reading the contents of this book; Total Quality involves everyone in the organization, in everything that they do at all times, forever! It is not a technical specialism, nor is it narrowly defined within product quality terms of system accreditation. It is about the total organization, involving everyone at all levels. For this reason, and because achieving Total Quality means meeting requirements which involve people in a chain-link process across functional and departmental boundaries, it is necessary to have a co-ordinating function. This co-ordinating function can be achieved by the Top Team with the help of a Total Quality manager.

The difficulties of co-ordinating departments and functions in an organization in such a way that the company meets the requirement agreed with the customer 100% of the time should not be underestimated. There is no chance of achieving success when the Top Team doesn't understand that the organizational design encourages compartmentalization between departments, to the detriment of meeting customer requirements. Even when they do there is so much work required to encourage and maintain good links between departments, that many Top Teams give up in desperation and frustration.

There is a strong case for providing a focus on co-ordination in the organization, by appointing a Total Quality manager. The role of the TQ manager needs to be very carefully defined. It may be seen by some members of the Top Team to be an opportunity to 'off-load' responsibility, or possibly even find a 'scapegoat' for failure. The Chief Executive must not allow this kind of thinking in his Top Team – it is clearly the responsibility of the whole Top Team to ensure the success of Total Quality in the organization. However, the use of a dedicated resource to provide planning, co-ordination and the necessary day-to-day support across the company is worth serious consideration.

Requirements for the Total Quality manager

The ideal would be a respected line manager with experience of the organization who is aware of the practical difficulties of implementing Total Quality. The person needs to have good interpersonal skills, and the ability to 'sell' the principles to people at every level.

Because of the need to look across the total organization, it is probable that familiarization with all parts of the organization is achieved <u>before</u> attempting to do the job. There is nothing worse than someone coming into a part of the organization which is unfamiliar to them and then attempting to tell everyone how to

Figure 13.2 'I wish they'd get out and help me!'

improve their jobs! It is both courteous and sensible to find out about the functions before getting involved. It will probably also be necessary for the TQ manager to become well versed in business and financial matters. This will ensure a good understanding of the need for a mission statement, business drivers and performance measures. A sound understanding of competitive benchmarking is essential, as is the ability to talk to both customers and suppliers.

Tools and techniques are the key to achieving successful problem solving and it follows, therefore, that the TQ manager must become an expert. It is no good knowing as much as everyone else on the TQ training courses, this is not enough. The requirement is to be capable of using complex problem solving tools such as multivari analysis, Taguchi, and SPC, Design of Experiment, relationship diagram etc. A particular requirement is the ability to flowchart the key processes across the organization – business process analysis.

As can be seen from the above it is not difficult to justify the appointment of a full-time Total Quality manager in most companies. It is very often used as a career move, albeit sideways many times, to help develop company and business knowledge in a key person, which will allow that person to take over a key Top Team role. This can be the Chief Executive or Managing Director's position, or a member of the Top Team dependent on the company requirements. However, it is an excellent career development opportunity as well as providing more resilience in the difficult process of implementing Total Quality successfully.

Providing the right person is appointed, the role is fully understood by the Top Team and the necessary plans are established and monitored, the TQ manager will be seen as a valuable and necessary addition to the Top Management team.

CHAPTER FOURTEEN

Summary

TQM requires careful planning and patient implementation. There can be no short cuts, and each step should be securely established before attempting to move on. The Top Team must lead and must be committed. Their adoption of the CEO's Quality Policy statement is a crucial foundation for the planning and implementation to rest upon.

The first step is to define the business strategy over a five-year period. As described earlier in the book, it is essential to determine a 'mission statement' for the business and the key 'business drivers' needed to achieve the mission. It is possible to integrate both the internal and external requirements for the business by recognizing the different customers the company has:

Internal : Shareholders, holding companies, financiers
External : Customers, marketplace

The mission statement should clearly define the products and services offered and the markets operated in, whilst ensuring that the company meet these external requirements at a profit.

The preceding Spenley Business Model shown in Figure 13.1 is useful for reminding the company CEO and Board of Directors that there are internal and external customer requirements to be met. It is essential to use the model to provide the understanding that the external requirements can only be met by taking different actions than is the case to begin with, and by making the necessary management time available to implement the transformation process into the company.

KEY BUSINESS PROCESSES

When the key business drivers have been agreed it is necessary to define the business processes associated with the drivers. The business processes always go across the organization which is the reason an internally-oriented organization has difficulty in control, since the organizational structure is vertical, as shown in Figure 14.1.

The business processes could be:

- On-time delivery performance
- On-time development of products/services
- Time to market
- Product Quality

These would be relatively easily defined by the company, following the establishment of its mission statement and business drivers, but it is a complex matter to define the processes across the organization.

BUSINESS PROCESS ANALYSIS

The analysis of key processes defines the departments and people involved, what their input and output requirements are

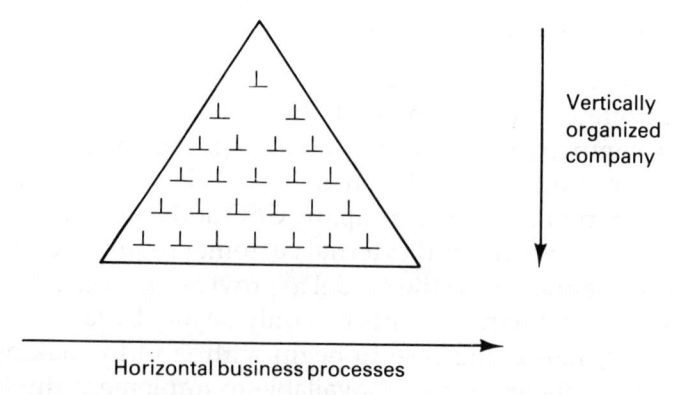

Figure 14.1 Horizontal processes – vertical organization.

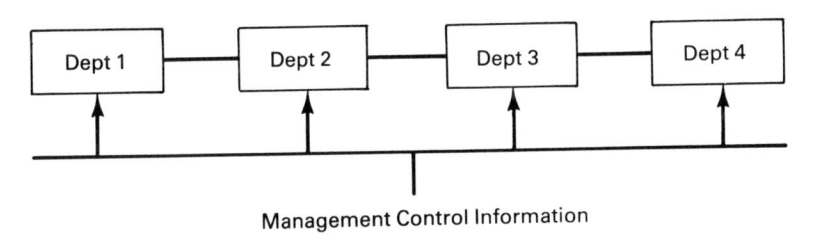

```
┌────────┐   ┌────────┐   ┌────────┐   ┌────────┐
│ Dept 1 ├───┤ Dept 2 ├───┤ Dept 3 ├───┤ Dept 4 │
└────────┘   └────────┘   └────────┘   └────────┘
     ▲            ▲            ▲            ▲
     │            │            │            │
─────┴────────────┴────────────┴────────────┴─────
                       │
            Management Control Information
```

Figure 14.2 The business process.

and the control mechanism which is required to ensure the process is effective.

From the diagram in Figure 14.2 it is clear that once the business process is defined it is possible to use the vertical organization hierarchy to control the total. With the implementation of the Total Quality process defined in earlier chapters of this book, everyone will clearly understand their requirements, have their own performance measures and be able to implement continuous improvement throughout the organization.

The structure of CATs and CITs ensure all problems can be addressed across the process whether they are multidisciplinary and therefore across departments, or whether applicable to one department.

This understanding of the key processes is why the Total Quality principles really work in an organization and is the beginning of the transformation from 'internal' to 'external' oriented focus.

PART THREE
Tools and techniques for TQM

Contents

1. Brainstorming
2. List reduction
3. Cause and effect analysis
4. Pareto analysis
5. Data collection techniques
6. Histograms
7. Flowcharts
8. Gantt charts
9. Failure mode analysis – guidelines
10. Ideas evaluation
11. Paired comparison
12. Why–Why diagram
13. How–How diagram

1. BRAINSTORMING

What is brainstorming?

Brainstorming is an idea-generating technique. A group of people throw out their ideas as they think of them, so that each has the opportunity to build on the ideas of others.

How to brainstorm

The group leader presents the situation for which ideas are sought. The wording should encourage specific, tangible ideas, not abstract ideas or opinions. The leader makes sure that the members understand the situation under consideration, the objective of the brainstorming session, and the process to be followed.

There are two methods of brainstorming. The most familiar is **free wheeling**, where:

- Group members call out their ideas spontaneously.
- The scribe records the ideas as they are suggested.

The discipline of brainstorming is maintained by four basic rules. However, the informality of the process generates an atmosphere of freedom. These rules are:

- No evaluation.
- Encourage wild ideas.
- Build on the ideas of others.
- Strive for quality.

In **round-robin** brainstorming,

- The leader or scribe asks each member, in turn, for an idea.
- Members may pass on any round.
- The session continues until all members have passed during the round.
- Ideas are recorded as in free wheeling.

Each approach has its advantages and disadvantages, but up to 80 ideas may be brainstormed. A way of reducing the number of items generated and evaluating them is called 'List Reduction'. This will help the team to concentrate on the most important items.

When to use brainstorming

To generate as many potential ideas as possible often in the context of cause and effect analysis.

Tips on improving the team's use of brainstorming

There are several recommended 'idea-spurring' questions to

1. BRAINSTORMING

Reasons why electric light doesn't turn on	
Power failure	Storm
Bulb loose	Power plant failure
Not plugged in	Old bulb
Lamp corroded	Broken bulb
No current to house	No contact
Bill not paid	Wall switch turned off
Bulb holder missing	Circuit breaker operated
Switch broken	Burnt out bulb
Cord cut	Missing bulb
Cord chewed by dog	Switch missing
Slot meter empty	

Figure A.1 An example of a brainstorm.

help group members build on each others' proposals. These questions could include:

1. What else is like this?
2. What other ideas does this suggest?
3. Greater frequency?

2. LIST REDUCTION

What is list reduction?

Before a list of ideas or factors can be shortened, everyone in the group must have a clear understanding of all items on the list. The first activity, therefore, is for the leader to go through the items asking if there is need for clarification. If yes, the suggester should be asked to briefly explain what he or she meant by the comment. The discussion should not go beyond simple clarification at this point.

How to list reduce

The group identifies some filters, criteria that should be satisfied for an item to remain in consideration, some of which could be:

- Is this item likely to improve the situation?
- Is it feasible?
- Can we afford it?

Keeping the agreed upon criteria in mind, group members review, or in appropriate cases vote on, each item. If there is any doubt items are bracketed, rather than crossed out, so that the group can go back to them later if necessary. In general the group focusses on and continues to evaluate only the non-bracketed items on the list.

The process may be repeated, with different or more stringent criteria, until the list is reduced to about half a dozen options. This represents a manageable number of options for applying some of the other evaluative tools.

When to use list reduction

List reduction is a filter technique. When used after brainstorming it is useful to combine it with a clarification process.

3. CAUSE AND EFFECT ANALYSIS (FISHBONE DIAGRAMS)

What is Cause and Effect analysis?

Cause and Effect diagrams are also known as 'fishbones' (because of their shape) or Ishikawa diagrams (after their inventor, Dr Kaoru Ishikawa, the Japanese Quality Control statistician).

Cause and Effect analysis is a systematic way of looking at effects and the causes that create or contribute to specified effects. The effect being analysed can be expressed as a problem or as 'desired state' and the things that have to be in place for us to get to where we want to be.

A fishbone is an organizing technique for processing lists of ideas into groups to make understanding clearer.

How to draw a Cause and Effect diagram

In order to provide a full analysis for any given effect, the causes can be represented on a cause and effect or fishbone diagram such as the one shown (Figure A.2) to illustrate the statement 'lamp doesn't turn on' and the major possible causes which might explain why the lamp doesn't light. Related causes are grouped together on bones of the fish which have been labelled with the common factor.

- Identify the area or 'effect' to be analysed or the desired state to be reached.
- Hold a brainstorming session with your team to establish all the major possible causes.
- Write the effect/desired state in a box at the end of the main spine of the fishbone. Add several bones, drawn at an angle.
- From the results of the brainstorming session form groups of causes under a number of headings comprising the main factors contributing to the effect being analysed.
- On each of the major bones, write the contributory factors which the group consider to be part of each cause.
- Then decide whether you need to collect additional data to further understand the relationships of cause to effect.

148   TOOLS AND TECHNIQUES FOR TQM

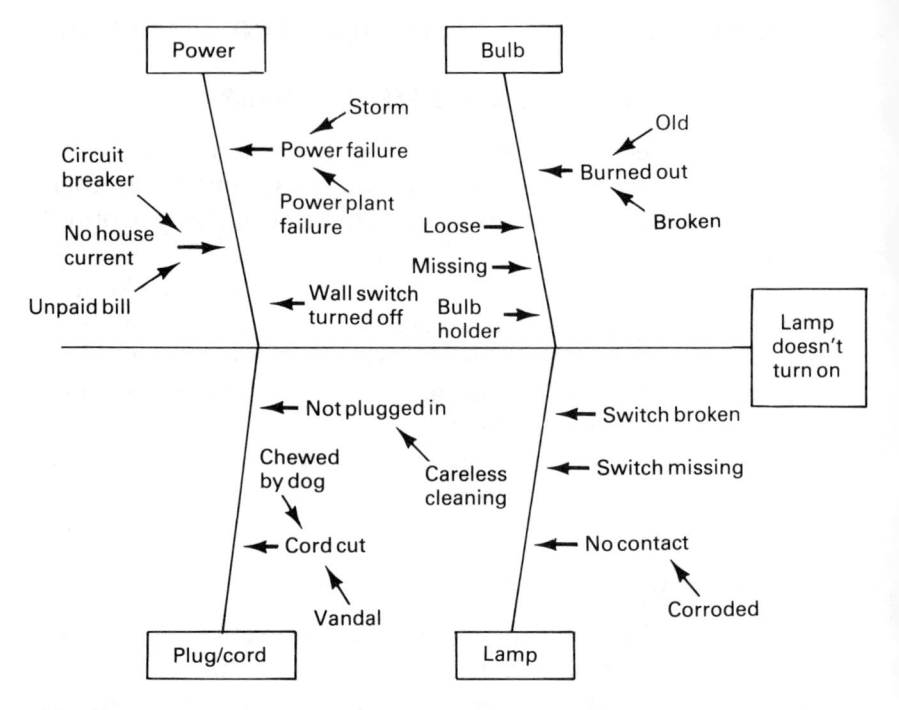

Figure A.2 An example of a cause and effect diagram.

ADDITIONAL TIPS FOR CONSTRUCTING THE CAUSE AND EFFECT DIAGRAMS

It is often the case that the following general headings apply:

Cause and Effect rules

1. Participation by everyone concerned is necessary to ensure that all causes are considered. Everyone involved, must be free to voice their ideas. The more ideas mentioned, the more accurate will be the diagram. One person's idea will trigger someone else's.
2. Do not criticize any ideas. To encourage a free exchange, write them all down. A brainstorming approach is often appropriate for these early steps.

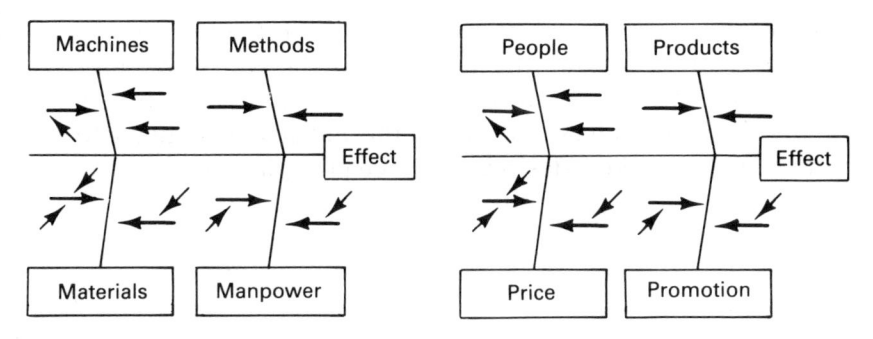

Figure A.3 Cause and Effect – additional tips.

3. Visibility is a major factor of participation. Everyone in the team must be able to see the diagram. Use large charts, large printing, and conduct the diagram sessions in a well-lit area.
4. Group together various causes which have a common theme or link and create a 'bone' for each theme.
5. Understand each cause as it is mentioned to ensure its proper placement on the diagram. Use the technique: Why, what, where, when, who and how.
6. Do not overload any one diagram. As a group of causes begins to dominate the diagram, that group should become a diagram itself.
7. Construct a separate diagram for each separate effect.
8. Circle the most likely causes. This is usually done after all possible ideas have been written up on the Cause and Effect diagram. Only then is each idea critically evaluated. The most likely ones should be circled for special attention.
9. Create an improvement-orientated atmosphere in each session. Focus on how to improve a situation rather than analysing how it arose.

When to use Cause and Effect diagrams

The Cause and Effect diagram has nearly unlimited application. One of its strongest attributes is the participation and contribution of everyone involved in the subject under discussion.

These diagrams are useful whenever a situation needs to be understood fully and the relationship between the various factors involved explored. This might be in the context of solving a problem or understanding all the areas which need to be addressed to make a desirable change take place.

4. PARETO ANALYSIS

What is Pareto analysis?

Pareto analysis is a technique for recording and analysing information which easily enables the most significant aspects to be identified. A pattern usually becomes apparent when we look at the relationship between the numbers of items/occurrences of any situation and their relation to the 'cause' under consideration. The pattern has been referred to as the '80/20 rule' and shows itself in many ways.

Pareto analysis shows at a glance which areas can be regarded as the 'vital few' needing priority measures to tackle them and which are the 'trivial many'.

The accomplishments of the Pareto analysis are:

- Some areas, previously not considered significant, are identified as belonging to the 'vital few'.

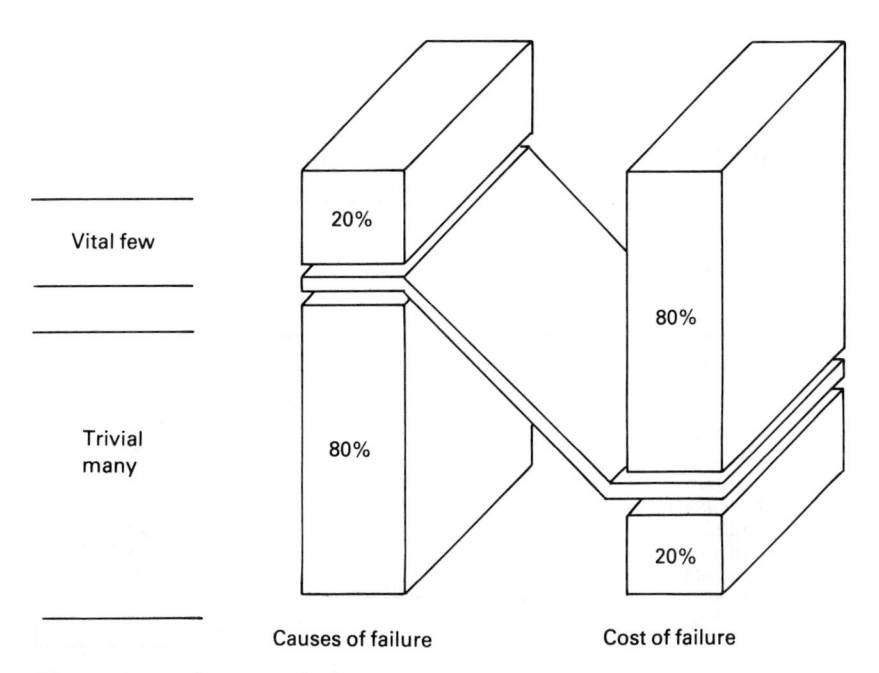

Figure A.4 Diagram showing the 80/20 rule.

- The 'trivial many' are identified: this is not new but the extent is usually surprising.
- Priorities are established.

How to construct a Pareto

Calculate totals

Taking information from a data or check sheet, list the items in rank order and calculate cumulative percentages. An analysis done in this manner relating to causes of mis-sorted mail is shown in Figure A.5.

Draw the Pareto diagram

Draw a bar chart which plots the cumulative percentage against the activities. It may be useful to group minor activities as 'others'. This is illustrated in Figure A.6.

Interpret the results

The candidates for priority action – the 'vital few' – will appear on the left of the Pareto diagram where the shape of the cumulative diagram will be steepest. The 'trivial many' should not be ignored, however, because sometimes what is apparently minor at first can become much more significant at a later date if it is left untreated.

Activity (failure)	Frequency	% of Total	Cumulative (%)
A. Poorly addressed	11	38	38
B. Wrongly addressed	9	31	69
C. Postroom error	4	14	83
D. Divisional error	2	7	90
E. No address	1	3.4	93.4
F. Item unreadable	1	3.3	96.7
G. Royal Mail error	1	3.3	100
TOTAL	29	100	100

Figure A.5 Pareto construction.

4. PARETO ANALYSIS

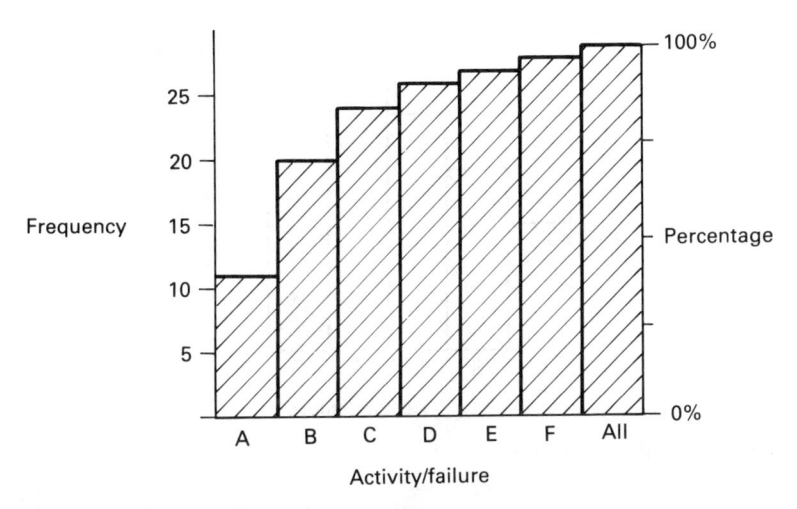

Figure A.6 Pareto diagram.

It is important when choosing the data to be charted to have a clear view of the ultimate purpose of the diagram. In the example given above if the purpose was to tackle those areas which most frequently caused failure then the correct data was charted. If the aim was to identify those activities which caused the greatest number of items to be mis-sorted the diagram could be quite different. Figure A.8 illustrates the revised ranking of the categories when this criterion is used.

Activity (failure)	Frequency	% of Total	Cumulative (%)
C. Postroom error	240	42	42
B. Wrongly addressed	109	19	61
D. Divisional error	106	18.5	79.5
A. Poorly addressed	76	13	92.5
G. Royal Mail error	41	7	99.5
F. Item unreadable	2	0.3	99.8
E. No address	1	0.2	100
TOTAL	575	100	100

Figure A.7 Pareto example.

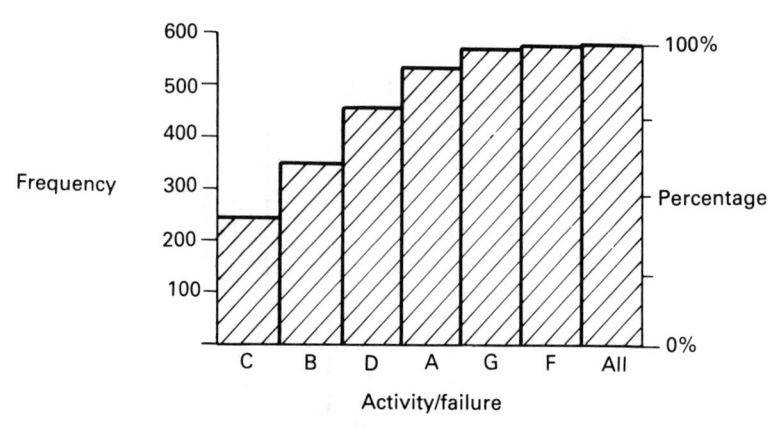

Figure A.8 Pareto chart.

When to use Pareto

Pareto can be used to great advantage in many situations where volumes of data exist. It assists with clarifying and prioritizing those aspects which warrant the commitment of resources in order to gain maximum advantage. Its major uses are in frequency based data and tracking that priorities remain the same even when volumes of data available varies widely.

5. DATA COLLECTION TECHNIQUES

In this section we are going to describe three data collection systems. Data sheets, frequency tables, and check sheets.

What are data sheets?
Data sheets are used to determine how often an event occurs over a designated period of time. Information is usually collected for events as they happen.

What are frequency tables?
Frequency tables are used to record the distribution of events within chosen boundaries.

What are check sheets?
Check sheets are used to record how often an event occurs.

Although the purpose of these techniques is to collect – not analyse – information, they can often help to indicate an area for action.

When to use data collection techniques

- To collect the information needed to analyse the present situation.
- To collect information needed to evaluate suggested courses of action.

Complaint	Jan	Feb	Mar	Apr	May	Jun	Jul	Aug	Sep	Oct	Nov	Dec	Total
Damaged Mail		11							1	111	11	ℋ̶ℋ̶	13

Figure A.9 An example of a data sheet.

Class Boundaries (lbs)	Frequencies
109.5–119.4	1
119.5–129.4	4
129.5–139.4	17
139.5–149.4	28
149.5–159.4	25
159.5–169.4	18
169.5–179.4	13
179.5–189.4	6
189.5–199.4	5
199.5–209.4	2
209.5–219.4	1
TOTAL	120

Figure A.10 Example of a frequency table. Distribution of the weight of 120 students.

TYPES OF TELEPHONE CALL	DEPARTMENT		
	Mails Branch	Personnel	Finance
Customer query	ℋ̶ℋ̶ ℋ̶ℋ̶	ℋ̶ℋ̶	ℋ̶ℋ̶ ℋ̶ℋ̶
Wrong numbers	ℋ̶ℋ̶ 1	1111	ℋ̶ℋ̶ ℋ̶ℋ̶ ℋ̶ℋ̶
Headquarters		11	1

Figure A.11 Example of a check sheet.

6. HISTOGRAMS

What is a histogram?

A histogram shows the distribution of some characteristic. Because of its immediate visual impact, a histogram is more effective than a table for displaying information.

How to Construct a histogram

- If the data is not already arranged by frequency make a frequency distribution table.
- Label the axis 'frequency' and mark values and units on it.
- Using the information in the frequency distribution table, construct vertical bars for each of the classes, with height corresponding to frequency.

An Example of a histogram

Data has been taken from the frequency distribution table in Figure A.10.

When to use histograms

Whenever appropriate to increase the visual impact of numerical data.

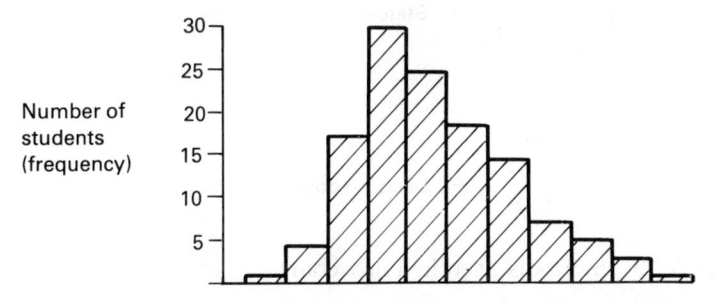

Weight range in pounds from 109.5 to 219.5 in 10 pound steps

Figure A.12 An example of a histogram.

7. FLOW CHARTS

What are flowcharts?

Flowcharts show the inputs, activities, decision points, and outputs for a given process. There are many variations that have been adapted for specific purposes (e.g. to show flow of paperwork through an administrative system; to show movement of materials through an operational system).

How to construct a flowchart

Flowcharts use standard symbols connected by arrows to show how the system or work process operates. To construct a flow chart, identify the major activites to be completed and decisions to be made as the work process is implemented. Then check the logic of the plan by following all possible routes through the chart to ensure that you have planned for contingencies.

Use the symbols shown in Figure A.13 when drawing a flow chart.

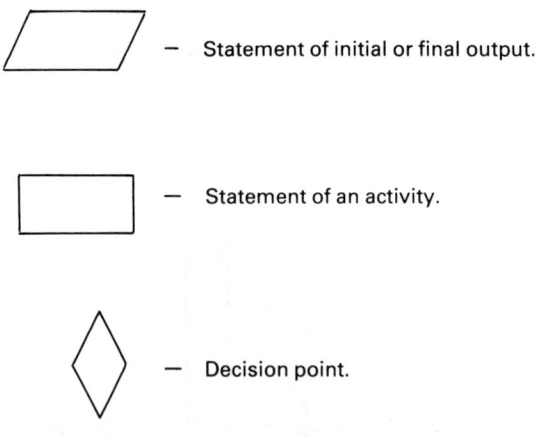

```
   /___/      — Statement of initial or final output.

   [___]      — Statement of an activity.

   <>         — Decision point.
```

Figure A.13 Symbols used in a flowchart.

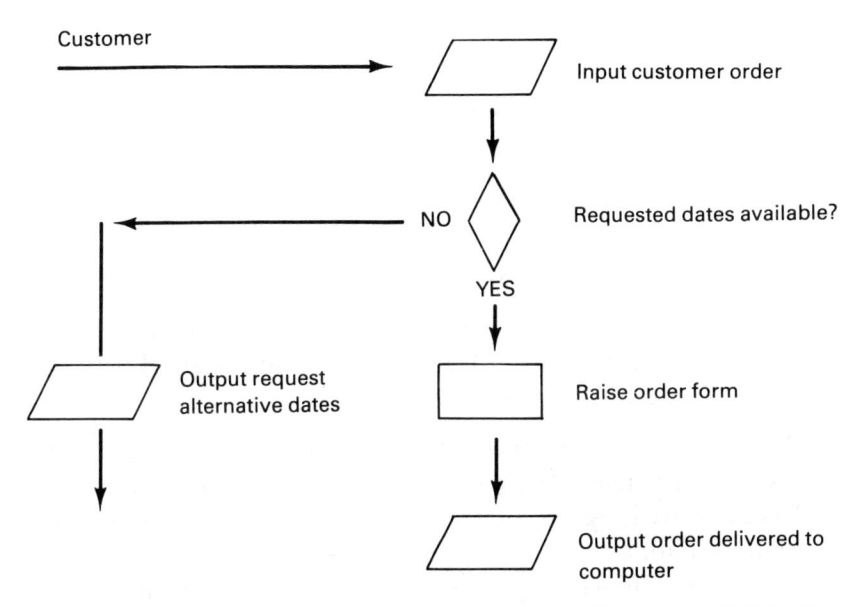

Figure A.14 An example of a flowchart. Responding to an HDS Order Enquiry.

When to use flowcharts

Flowcharts are particularly useful for documenting the steps of a work process either to analyse the current situation or to provide a plan to follow.

8. GANTT CHARTS

What are Gantt charts?

A Gantt chart is a diagram that documents the schedule, events, activities, and responsibilities necessary to complete a project.

How to construct a Gantt chart

Although there are many variations, all Gantt charts document what is to be accomplished, by whom, and when. The steps required to construct a Gantt chart are:

- Break the implementation plan into achievable steps.
- Assign responsibility for each step to a team member.
- Decide how long each task will take, and set a realistic completion date.
- Document the assumptions on which the plan is based, and the contingency plans to implement if those assumptions are not valid.

When to use Gantt charts

Gantt charts are particularly useful when managing a complex multi-phased task or where the aim is to optimize the use of resources or manpower.

SCHEDULE

Task	Assigned to	Week ending							
		1/6	8/6	15/6	22/6	29/6	5/7	12/7	19/7
Liaise with districts	Andrew								
Process bids	Helen								
Discuss bids with MT	Helen								
Discuss van movement	Peter								
Deploys vans	Peter and Helen								

Figure A.15 An example of the use of a Gantt chart, using a transport project.

9. FAILURE MODE EFFECT ANALYSIS – GUIDELINES

1. List part/process under consideration, e.g. gear.
2. For each part/process list all possible failure modes, e.g. fracture, excess vibration.
3. List possible effects of failure, e.g. gearbox failure, increased maintenance etc.
4. List possible causes of failure, e.g. material, heat treatment, incorrect gear form etc.
5. Probability factor – assess how likely failure is. Base on reliability data if possible, if not use best judgement.
   1 = Failures extremely infrequent.
   10 = Failures almost certain to occur.
6. Severity factor – assume failure has occurred. Will this have impact on customer? Assume also the customer will get the defect.
   1 = Customer will not notice.
   10 = Safety of product affected.
7. Detection factor – what is the probability the customer will subsequently receive the product?
   1 = Will not reach the customer.
   10 = Customer will receive product.
8. Multiply together to obtain risk factor (improvement weighing).

10. IDEAS EVALUATION

Purpose

To identify ideas that the team can work on.

Method

Take the brainstorm lists and evaluate and categorize each idea into one of the following groups; mark up the lists with the appropriate capital letter indicated below:

- T = Totally within the team's control to work on, and to be able to produce a solution to the problem which is likely to be implemented.
- P = Partially controllable within the group, i.e. the team may be able to come up with some solution, but the total problem would probably need the involvement of other departments.
- N = Not team controllable as are ideas over which the group has no direct control at all, e.g. redesign the building.

- During this process it may be appropriate to cross out any ideas which are totally superfluous.
- Take all the 'T' type items and decide which one the team members would like to tackle (note in many cases it will be appropriate to do a data gathering exercise first, to measure which is the most significant problem).

11. PAIRED COMPARISON

Purpose

- To get group consensus on the selection of an item from a list (e.g. which problem shall we tackle?).
- To avoid problems with voting systems.

Rules

- Each member does his or her own chart.

Method

- List all contending items (in any order) on the left.
- Compare item 1 with item 2 – decide which is the most important and ring the appropriate number in column 1 row 1.
- Repeat, comparing item 1 with item 3 etc. and ring the appropriate number in each succeeding column.
- Then after item 1 has been compared with all the others, go on to item 2 and repeat the cycle of events until all items have had a paired comparison.
- Count up all the ringed '1's on the chart and put the total against item 1. Do this for all the other numbers.
- Use the Vote Matrix to record the votes for each item from each member's chart. Add the votes across each row to find out the circle's total score for each item.
- The maximum score will identify the major item to look at first.

11. PAIRED COMPARISON 165

No.	ITEM							
1		1 2	1 3	1 4	1 5	1 6	1 7	1 8
2		2 3	2 4	2 5	2 6	2 7	2 8	
3		3 4	3 5	3 6	3 7	3 8		
4		4 5	4 6	4 7	4 8			
5		5 6	5 7	5 8				
6		6 7	6 8					
7		7 8						
8								

VOTE MATRIX FOR PAIRED COMPARISONS

No.	Member votes	Totals	Ranking
1			
2			
3			
4			
5			
6			
7			
8			

Figure A.16 Paired comparison chart.

12. WHY–WHY DIAGRAM

Purpose

- To provide an alternative method of identifying root causes to a problem.
- To practice divergent thinking technique.

Rules

- Brainstorm the causes.
- Identify the major cause.

Method

- Take a selected cause and use a WHY–WHY diagram to explore the underlying causes of the problem.
- Each divergent step of the WHY–WHY analysis is produced asking 'why?', as shown in Figure A.17.
- The answers to the question 'why?' are causes of the problem.

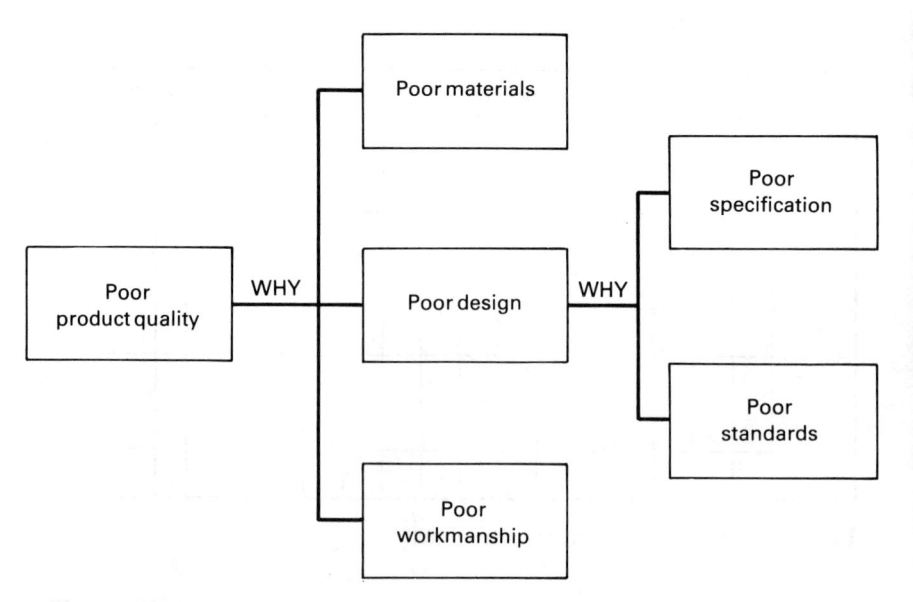

Figure A.17 Example of Why–Why diagram.

13. HOW–HOW DIAGRAM

Purpose

- To creatively explore and consider numerous solution alternatives instead of jumping to the 'obvious solution'.
- Helps members determine the specific steps that should be taken to implement a solution and hence formulate a specific action plan.
- It helps practice a divergent technique.

Method

- Begin with a solution statement and explore possible ways of accomplishing the action at each stage by asking 'how?' (Figure A.18).
- At each stage of the chain a convergent process can be used to narrow the list of alternatives before the next divergent step is taken.
- Advantages and disadvantages, change of success, and relative cost of each alternative can be established to get a more objective selection process.

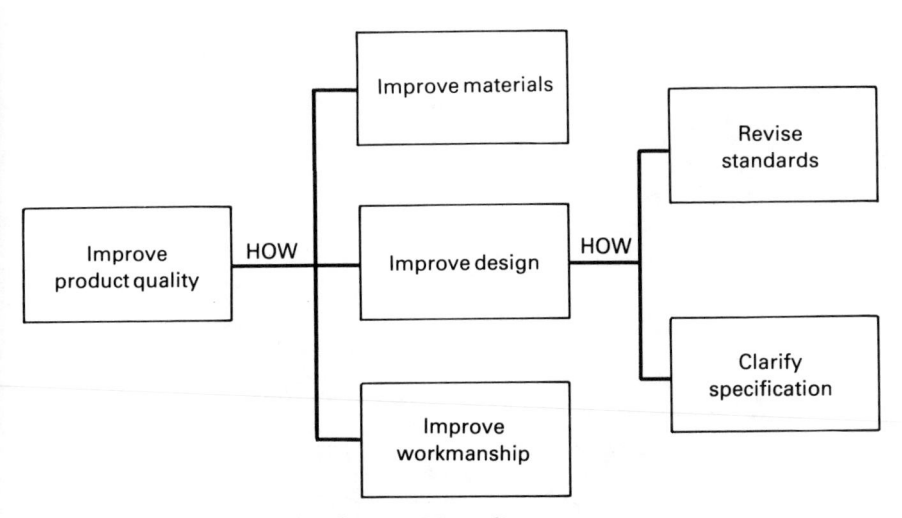

Figure A.18 Example of How–How diagram.

Index

'Analysis paralysis' 34
Attitudes 22
Audit of customers 49

British Institute of Management (BIM) 12
Benchmarking 48
Brainstorming 90, 143
Brand loyalty 52
Business
   drivers 16, 47, 137
   processes 138
   requirements 15, 47
   strategy 14, 137

Cascade 80
Capability 25
Cause and effect analysis 83, 147
Certificate of achievement 114
Champions, see Quality champions
Commitment 13, 52, 68, 107
   see also Management commitment
Communication 53, 77
   methods 108
   timing 107
Competitive analysis 47
Computer Integrated Manufacture (CIM) 11

Consensus management 31, 44
Continuous improvement
   attitude 24
   policy 52
   team 88
Corrective action 35
   team 88
Cost
   of conformance 31, 82
   of non-conformance 31
   of total quality 31, 64, 80, 88
   trends 81
Culture 6, 85, 110, 128, 130
Customers
   audit, see Audit of customers
   internal 22
   external 137
Customer/supplier concept 21

Data collection 155
Deming, Dr E. 6
Design and development 125
Design of experiments (DOE) 80
Drivers, see Business drivers

Education 93
External focus 131

INDEX

Field trial 126
Financial support 67
'Firefighting' 27, 109
'Fishbone diagrams', see Cause and effect analysis
'Fix-it' mentality 27
Flowcharts 158
Failure Mode Effects Analysis (FMEA) 162
Flexible Manufacturing Systems (FMS) 12

Gantt charts 160
GOYA 109, 111

Histogram 156
How–How diagram 167

Ideas evaluation 163
Improvement
  see Continuous improvement
  process cycle 35
Internal customers and suppliers, see Customer/supplier concept
Information Technology (IT) 12
Involvement 78, 107
Ishikawa, K. 147

Japanese Union of Scientists and Engineers (JUSE) 6
Juran, Dr J. 6

Launch of TQM 107, 108
List reduction 146

Management
  commitment 66
  consensus, see Consensus management
  role 111
  style 109
Master in Business Administration (MBA) 10
Market
  requirements 124
  research 10
Mature product requirement 127
Measurement 54, 76
  systems and equipment 82
Mission statement 45, 137

Nissan 3, 7
Nobel prizes 12
Non-conformance, see Cost of total quality

Objectives of business 10
'Open market', see 'Single market'
Organizational design 128

Paired comparison 164
Pareto analysis 151
Performance measures, see Measurement
Prevention 26, 105
Principles of TQM 19
Problem solving 98
  cycle 99, 123
  log 105
  system 104
Product
  definition 125
  introduction 121
Profit sharing 114

Quality
  circles 85, 89
  champions 109
  control 20
  costs, see Cost of total quality

INDEX

culture, see Culture
definition 20
improvement cycle 36
improvement teams 65, 85
of customer service 74
of information 42
of management 41
of organization 43
perception 19
policy 40, 64, 71
of products and services 44
of systems 42

Recognition and reward 67, 110, 111, 113
Requirements 20
Rolls Royce 16
Root causes 27

Scientific management 4
Service
  industries x
  functions x
Share ownership scheme 114
'Single market' ix
Spenley
  Business process 132
  Business management process 55
Statistical Process Control (SPC) 80
Strategy, see Business strategy

Status 23
Structure of Total Quality Management (TQM) 65
Supplier
  assessment process 118
  definition 116
  status 118
  strategy 116

Taguchi 80
Taylor, F.W. 4
Team indicator chart 79
Technology 11
Time to market 120
Tools and techniques 28, 143
Top-down approach 56
Top team 28, 56, 87, 95, 108, 137
Total Quality Control (TQC) 6
Total Quality Manager 133
Training 16
  facilities 97
  for problem solving 98
  structure 93
  planning 95

Why–Why diagram 166

Zero defects (ZD) 25